A GUIDE TO
WORK-HOLDING
ON THE LATHE

A GUIDE TO
WORK-HOLDING
ON THE LATHE

Fred Holder

GUILD OF MASTER CRAFTSMAN PUBLICATIONS

First published 2004 by
Guild of Master Craftsman Publications Ltd
166 High Street, Lewes
East Sussex, BN7 1XU

ISBN 1 86108 395 5

British Cataloguing in Publication Data
A catalogue record of this book is available from the
British Library.

Publisher: Paul Richardson
Art Director: Ian Smith
Managing Editor: Gerrie Purcell
Commissioning Editor: April McCroskie
Production Manager: Stuart Poole
Editor: Gill Parris
Designer: Fineline Studios

Typeface: Redford

Colour reproduction by Icon Reproduction
Printed and bound by Stamford Press Pte Ltd, Singapore.

Credits

Photographs

All photographs were taken by the author, with the exception of:

Front cover, main picture
Anthony Bailey

Front cover, top row, supplied courtesy of:
Oneway Manufacturing (left)
Record Power Limited (centre and far right)

Back cover: Courtesy of Oneway Manufacturing

Other photographs were supplied courtesy of the following manufacturers:
Axminster Power Tool Centre, pp. 77 and 78
Beall Tool Company; p. 59 (bottom right)
Oneway Manufacturing, pp. 69, 70 and 71
Record Power Limited pp. 82–3
Sierra Mold, p. 95
Vicmarc, pp. 73 and 75
Woodchucker's Supplies, p. 107

Illustrations

All illustrations by Simon Rodway, with the exception of the following, supplied by:

Multistar Woodturning Systems, pp. 21 (top) and 50
Teknatool International, p. 62
Professor Johannes Volmer, Germany, p. 109

Contents

Why this Book was Written

The idea for this book came about as a result of a lot of questions posted on a 'Usenet' discussion group, seeking information about the various methods of holding work on the lathe. I, and others, had answered many of these questions time and again, but there were still more. Then came a lengthy discussion on the vacuum chuck. One of the posters suggested that someone should write a book on the vacuum chuck and pull all of this information together for others to share. This prompted me to consider the many questions concerning how work can be held on the lathe. I did not feel that the vacuum chuck would provide enough basis for an entire book, but I did think it would make a good chapter in a book on different methods of holding the work on the lathe. I sent a letter off to the publisher suggesting such a book. Their response was positive. That was the beginnings of *A Guide to Work-holding on the Lathe*.

Safety Procedures

Although woodturning is safer than many other activities involving machinery, bear in mind that all machine work is inherently dangerous unless suitable precautions are taken.

Do not use timber which may come apart on the lathe – beware of faults such as dead knots, splits, shakes, loose bark, and so on.

Avoid loose clothing or hair which may catch in machinery. Protect your eyes and lungs against dust and flying debris by wearing goggles, dust mask or respirator as necessary, but invest in an efficient dust extractor as well.

Pay attention to electrical safety; in particular, do not use wet sanding or other techniques involving water unless your lathe is designed so that water cannot come into contact with the electrics.

Keep tools sharp; blunt tools are dangerous because they require more pressure and may behave unpredictably.

It is not safe to use a chainsaw without the protective clothing which is specially designed for this purpose, and attendance on a recognized training course is strongly recommended. Be aware that regulations governing chainsaw use are revised from time to time.

Do not work when your concentration is impaired by drugs, alcohol or fatigue.

The safety advice in this book is intended for your guidance, but cannot cover every eventuality: the safe use of machinery and tools is the responsibility of the user. If you are unhappy with a particular technique or procedure, do not use it – there is always another way.

1 Introduction to the Lathe and The History of Chucking

The function of the lathe is to hold the wood and make it revolve, so that a woodturner can hold a chisel across a toolrest and carve the rotating wood. But, before I give detailed descriptions of the different methods of holding work on the lathe, I would like to look at the evolution of the lathe and, along with it, the methods of holding work on the lathe for turning.

No one knows when the lathe actually came into use, but it is thought that the early Egyptians were responsible for its development. Those early lathes were probably powered by a string wrapped around the workpiece and attached to each end of a bowed piece of wood, usually a limb or branch. By moving the bow back and forth, the workpiece was caused to rotate. This was probably a natural evolution from the fire drill or bow drill (I have no idea which came first), which is thought to have preceded the lathe. The bowstring was wrapped around a drill shaft; the drill shaft was suspended between the work being drilled and a hand-held support at the top and, by moving the bow back and forth the drill was caused to rotate and drill a hole in the workpiece.

If the piece of wood to be turned was suspended by points on each end in a horizontal position, the turner could sit in front of this suspended piece of wood and cut it with his chisel when the wood was rotated towards him. The bow could be used to rotate the wood, as it did the drill with the bow drill.

These lathes were extremely simple and consisted of two points embedded in a log or a post set in the ground. The workpiece was mounted between centres with the string of the bow making one or more wraps around it. When the bow was moved, the wood would rotate between the centres (see Fig 1.1).

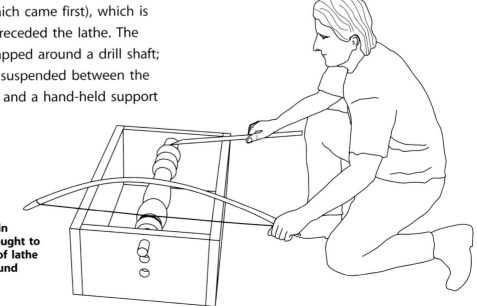

Fig 1.1 **A bow lathe in operation. This is thought to be the earliest form of lathe for making things round**

The Bow Lathe

The bow lathe is very simple to use and is still used today in some of the more primitive societies, and by some jewellers on small jewellers' lathes. Often, the operator of the lathe moves the bow and controls the chisel with one hand, or one hand and a foot.

This simple lathe would seem to be a natural basis for the development of the pole lathe which, apparently, came into use more than 500 years ago. The pole lathe was used extensively in the woods to turn furniture pieces at the site of felling the tree until the late 1930s or early 1940s (these guys were called bodgers), and it is still used today by some custom furniture makers.

The Pole Lathe

For the pole lathe, a framework was constructed to hold the wood at a height that would enable the operator to stand in front of it to work. The bow was replaced by a springy pole overhead – usually a sapling – to which one end of the cord was attached. The cord was brought down, wrapped one or more times about the workpiece, and continued on down to a foot pedal on the floor. The operator depressed the pedal, which pulled the thong down and rotated the wood towards the operator, so that he might make a cut with his chisel. When the pedal reached the floor, the operator released the pressure from his foot and the springy pole reversed the rotation of the workpiece, and raised the foot pedal for

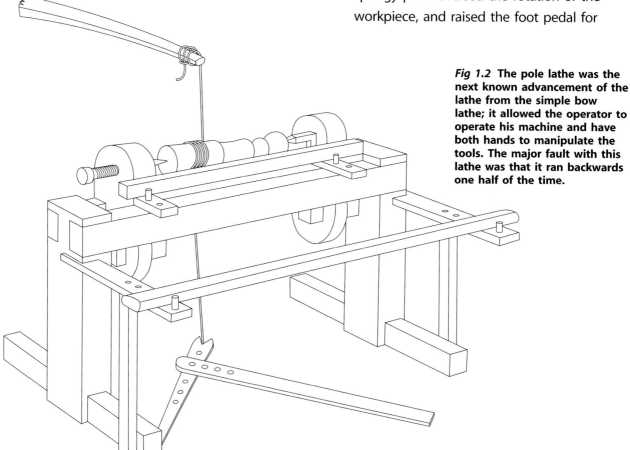

Fig 1.2 **The pole lathe was the next known advancement of the lathe from the simple bow lathe; it allowed the operator to operate his machine and have both hands to manipulate the tools. The major fault with this lathe was that it ran backwards one half of the time.**

another cycle. The operator could only turn wood half of the time and had to remove the tool from the wood for the reverse rotation. Fig 1.2 (opposite) shows the details of a pole lathe. There were many variations of spring used for these lathes; the simplest was a springy pole, while some of the more sophisticated used a bow with multiple strings and a pulley to allow more travel in a given amount of space.

The pole lathe was easiest to use for spindle work, such as that required by the furniture industry. However, it could also be used to turn bowls – which were basically turned between centres – with a portion of the bowl blank turned to form a pulley for the cord to drive it. It was also possible to use a spindle with metal prongs that could be driven into one side of the bowl blank;

the cord was then wound around this spindle to rotate the bowl blank for turning. The operator used hook tools to core the bowl into several bowls – which were only separated after the bowl was removed from the lathe – and the foot and the inside base of the bowl were then finished by hand, off the lathe.

The Great Wheel Lathe

Apparently, at the same time as the pole lathe was being developed, the great wheel lathe appeared on the scene. This lathe uses a large wheel separated from the lathe as the power unit. The wheel had several steps on it to hold the cord, which was a complete circle running from the great wheel to a pulley on the lathe.

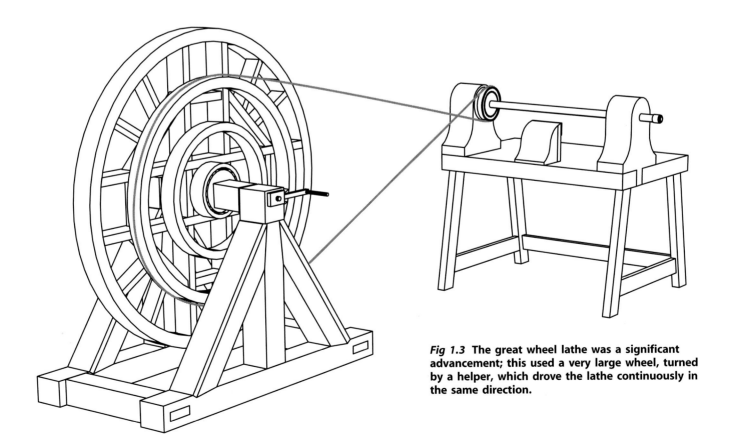

Fig 1.3 The great wheel lathe was a significant advancement; this used a very large wheel, turned by a helper, which drove the lathe continuously in the same direction.

An apprentice would turn the great wheel with a hand crank and power was transferred to the lathe by the cord. The advantage of this was that the wood rotated continuously in the direction required for cutting, but it did take up considerable space. A great wheel lathe is shown in Fig 1.3, on the previous page.

From the technology evolved to create the great wheel lathe, it was a small step to placing the wheel (a much smaller one) onto the lathe itself, and operating it by a foot pedal and a crank mechanism; this again made the lathe self-contained, and it was operated by a single person. Such a lathe is shown in Figure 1.4, below.

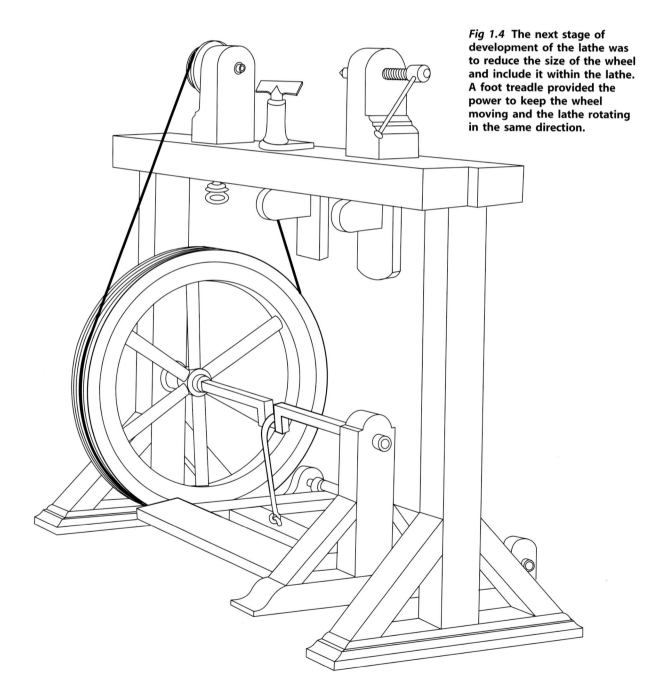

Fig 1.4 The next stage of development of the lathe was to reduce the size of the wheel and include it within the lathe. A foot treadle provided the power to keep the wheel moving and the lathe rotating in the same direction.

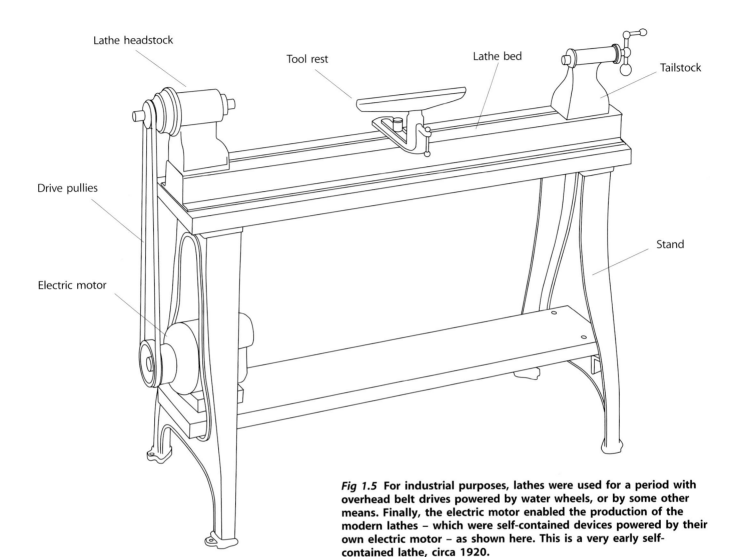

Lathe headstock

Tool rest

Lathe bed

Tailstock

Drive pullies

Stand

Electric motor

Fig 1.5 **For industrial purposes, lathes were used for a period with overhead belt drives powered by water wheels, or by some other means. Finally, the electric motor enabled the production of the modern lathes – which were self-contained devices powered by their own electric motor – as shown here. This is a very early self-contained lathe, circa 1920.**

It is interesting to note that, as late as 1816, the more elaborate portable lathes were still provided with both a wheel for continuous rotation and with a bow for operation in the spring-pole mode.

Power-operated Lathes

Factories often used water power or steam power to drive complex overhead drive systems, and lathes operated in this way reduced the fatigue of the operator and speeded up production.

It wasn't until the wide introduction of electricity and the inexpensive electric motor that the lathes in small shops gave up their treadles for power, and the modern lathe with its self-contained power was introduced. A lathe with an electric motor is shown in Figure 1.5, above.

With the creation of continuous rotation and a rotating headstock mandrel, or spindle driven by a pulley, other means of mounting the workpiece could be devised besides the simple between-centres mounting required by the bow lathe and the spring-pole lathes.

By threading the mandrel, a number of different drive items could be mounted onto the end of the mandrel. The earliest was probably a drive centre for between-centres mounting of the workpiece. However, since much of the material that needed to be turned, whether metal or wood, could best be done by mounting it on the mandrel without the support of a tail centre, faceplates appeared, as did a number of other forms of work-holding devices. For woodturning, these devices were often made of wood, and were made by the lathe operator himself to meet the needs of a specific job. One of the commonly used devices or chucks was the spring (or compression) chuck, shown in Figure 1.6.

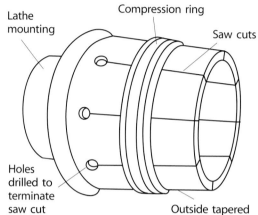

Fig 1.6 **One of the common ways of mounting the workpieces that were held on only one end was the spring (or compression) chuck, shown here.**

The Spring (or Compression) Chuck

This chuck is just as useful today as it was in the 1800s and I know several woodturners who regularly make one up to hold work for a specific production project. Since these chucks cannot be purchased anywhere, it seems appropriate to include information on making them here.

These chucks generally had a hole turned to the specified diameter, a turned-down section, which had been sawn through to cut it into eight or more segments, and a

clamping device – such as a ring – to compress the segments onto the item it was designed to hold. They served turners for many years and can still be used quite effectively, although they are not as handy as the modern scroll chuck, nor do they have the holding power of the modern chucks. They are, however, inexpensive and easy to make, and ideal for small delicate projects.

Several years ago, I had need for a spring chuck to hold something for finish turning – I've long since forgotten what. I made that first one by mounting a block of hard maple on a faceplate, turning the necessary hole, turning down the area over the hole to a wall thickness of about ⅛in (3mm), sawing it into eight segments and then, in place of a ring, I used a hose clip that I had in my toolbox as a compressible ring. A ring is smooth, but the hose clip can do some knuckle-knocking if you don't exercise care. Anyway, it worked quite well.

The main problem with this approach is that it ties up a faceplate. However, if the chuck is recessed at the back to fit the faceplate, it can be removed and put back so that it fits exactly. I used a piece of wood, and recessed the back to suit the size of the faceplate.

I subsequently purchased a couple of Nova scroll chucks and discontinued use of these home-made spring chucks. However, I made a spring chuck for use on my foot-powered lathe to hold 1in (25mm) dowel stock. It worked well enough, so I decided to make others to hold several smaller–sized spigots; i.e. ⅝in, ½in, ⅜in (16mm, 13mm, 10mm). They worked well on the foot-powered lathe and looked just right for it. They also work well on regular lathes, as long as you exercise care to avoid the spinning hose clip.

If you don't have a chuck to fit the job at hand, you can always make up a home-made spring chuck from a scrap of firewood, a small faceplate that fits your spindle, and a hose clip. There is not really any size limitation to this and, if you are worried about having to keep taking off and fitting the faceplate, you can always make up a special faceplate for your chuck that has a metal plate welded to a nut. We look at making faceplates later on (see page 23).

To Make a Spring/Compression Chuck:

1 First, select a suitable piece of wood in which the grain runs parallel to the axis of rotation of the lathe – maple, sycamore or fruitwoods are ideal. The wood must be of a sufficient size to fit your job and to allow the faceplate to be recessed into it. Mount a faceplate to one end, and fix it onto your lathe spindle.

2 Turn the block round, and drill or turn a recess to fit your faceplate, about ¼–⅜in (6–10mm) deep; it should be a snug fit – this will locate the faceplate each time. Take the faceplate off the lathe, unscrew the wood from it, then locate the faceplate in the recess, screw into position, and remount it on the spindle.

3 Next, drill or turn a parallel hollow to suit the size of workpiece to be held by the chuck: the workpiece should

just fit into the hollow. You can also create a step at the front internal section so that the back shoulder of the step acts as a registration point for items such as coat pegs and draughts pieces. If you use a drill to start this recess, drill right through the wood – you may need to push a rod through this hole to push your workpiece free from the chuck.

Warning

When hollowing, avoid going too deep and hitting the screws.

4 Once the internal hollow has been turned, turn down the outside to create a taper, with a front nose-section wall thickness of about ⅛–¼in (3–6mm). N.B. If you make it too thin, the chuck will be weak at this point, too thick and the chuck will not compress properly.

5 Next, saw approximately eight equal-length slits (if it is a fairly large diameter, use more than eight). I use a dovetail saw, or the bandsaw, and finish to the required depth with the dovetail saw. Either way, you want to cut down to just before the bottom of the hollow and, once cut, drill a hole at the end of each slit to prevent splitting. At this point, I generally oil my new chuck – simply because it makes it look better. Slip on the hose clip, and you have a new spring chuck ready to go.

Warning

The hose clip can rap knuckles and damage them if you are not careful. A large, wide, elastic band or piece of tyre inner tube placed over the clamp provides some protection. Taping over the clip with insulation tape is even better. Alternatively, turn a simple ring that has a tapered inner hole to match the taper on the cup chuck, and use that instead of the hose clip.

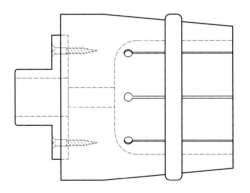

Fig 1.7 **Side view of the chuck, showing the internal hollow, fixings, and knocking-out hole**

Note: make sure that you have turned the stepped-down part sufficiently small to fit the clamp you have available, while the chuck is still on the lathe.

Today, when a lathe is purchased, it generally comes with a drive centre, a tail centre and a faceplate. The remainder of this chapter is devoted to these items, and the items that are available from other suppliers, and work better in some instances.

Drive Centres

Drive centres are usually installed into the headstock spindle with a Morse taper and can have two, four or more spurs (prongs or blades) to grab the wood – hence 'spur drive' – in addition to a sharp-pointed centre. The point of the centre generally contacts the wood before the blades do, to allow insertion of the point into a previously marked indent, or onto a centre mark on the wood. As the name implies, the purpose of this centre is to drive the wood when the lathe is switched on, as well as hold it in position when another centre located in the tailstock presses the wood against the drive centre.

Drive centres come in a number of different shapes and configurations, some of which are shown in Fig 1.8 (right): the Stebcenter, which has a spring-loaded centre and a ring of little points to grab the wood; the four-spur drive centre (usually supplied with a lathe), and a ring or cup centre.

When using the spur centre or a two-spur chisel centre, saw cuts may be made in the end of the wood to help the blades to grip the wood without splitting it, as this allows the wood to be held with less tailstock pressure and less strain on the wood; it is also a wise precaution, because certain woods sometimes crack or split out when the drive centre is pressed into the wood with just tailstock pressure. Also, with these drive centres, a major catch with the chisel will often tear the wood from the lathe and damage the drive-end beyond repair.

Fig 1.8 **A selection of drive centres (from left): Stebcenter, four-spur drive centre, ring or cup centre**

There are other spindle drive centres that are worthy of mention, but they are mostly for special applications. Square drive centres have a tapered, square hole in the end that will drive small, square stock up to about ½in (13mm) square. These are generally referred to as lace bobbin drives and provide self-centring of small square spindles (see Fig 1.9).

Preventing a Mishap

One way for beginners to prevent such a mishap is to use a cup-type centre – which is designed for use in the tailstock – as the drive centre. These centres have a sharp ring, that cuts into the wood, as well as a centre pin. With such a drive, a catch will simply stop the wood while causing little or no damage. It does require a light touch with the tool, and this will help a beginner turner to develop the light touch required for most spindle turning.

Fig 1.9 **Other forms of drive mechanism for between-centres turning (from left): bottle stopper drive centre; two different square drive centres, used to drive small, square pieces (such as lace bobbin blanks); stepped drive for use in turning light pulls.**

Another special-purpose drive is a light-pull drive, which serves as a friction drive and requires considerable tailstock pressure. This drive has a number of steps ranging from about 1/8–1/2in (3–13mm), and a hole is drilled in one end of the piece to be turned to fit one of these steps. The workpiece then fits onto that step, and is pressed against a tapered area at the rear of the step to provide friction-drive of the workpiece. Normally, on light pulls, a larger hole is drilled in the bottom of the pull to hold the knot, and a smaller hole is drilled all of the way through for the pull-string; this enables the turning of a workpiece that is exactly centred on the holes.

Tail Centres

The tail centre provides a second, movable centre point for the mounting of wood between centres for turning. Its basic purpose is to support the end of a spindle that is being driven by the centre in the headstock, and to apply pressure against the headstock drive centre while turning. Tail centres consist of two basic types: the dead centre and the rotating (or live) centre.

A number of years ago, lathes came with a dead centre very similar to the dead centres used with metal-cutting lathes. Such centres worked fine, but you did need to lubricate the centre and the hole that it ran in with a bit of wax or grease to prevent wear and burning. This problem has mostly been eliminated by the modern revolving centres, which have a bearing between the mounting Morse taper and the centre, allowing the centre to rotate freely with the wood. For most purposes, these are a great step forward, but they have introduced a bit of wobble – even though you can't see it, there is always a bit of play in a set of bearings. Hence, if you are doing extremely precise work, a dead centre with a little wax will give you more precise support. Fig 1.10 shows several tail centres that are available on the market.

The two live centres with which I am most familiar are the Oneway Revolving Centre, manufactured in Canada, and the Nova Revolving Centre, manufactured in New Zealand. Both of these have replaceable centres in different configurations, and the centre may be removed to allow the drilling of deep holes through the tailstock, such as for lamp-making. There are a number of others on the market that I have not had the opportunity to use.

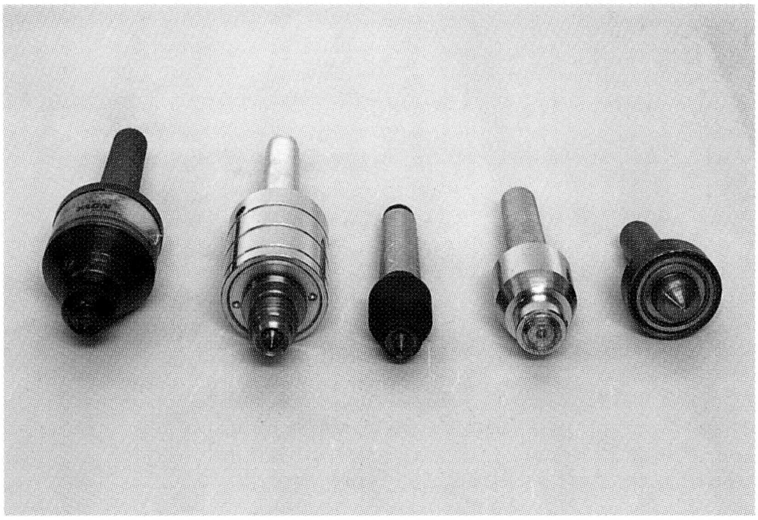

Fig 1.10 **Selection of tail centres (from left): Nova live centre; Oneway live centre; Oneway cup centre (dead centre); a commercial live centre with easily changeable centres held in place with a magnet; Nova DVR 3000 live tailcentre, furnished with the lathe.**

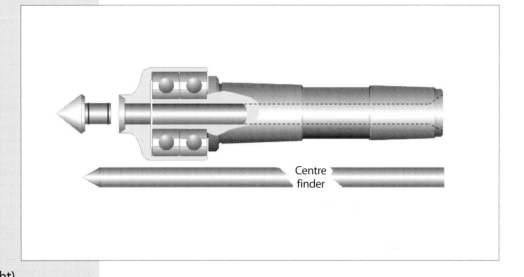

Centre finder

Faceplates

Almost all new lathes are supplied with one or more faceplates as a standard accessory (see Fig 1.11). Faceplates are designed so that you can attach a piece of wood for turning, without the need for a tailstock support. It is, however, a good idea to support large, out-of-balance chunks of wood with the tailstock until they are turned round and are more balanced.

The faceplate consists of a centre hub with a thread to fit your lathe spindle; it has a recess at the rear of the threads which allows the faceplate to screw onto the threads until the rear mates with the machined flange on the headstock spindle – this is necessary to ensure the faceplate runs true when it is removed and then replaced – and the front of the faceplate should be parallel to this mating surface.

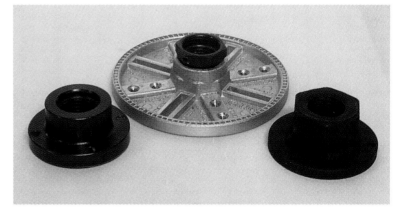

Fig 1.11 A selection of faceplates (from left): the faceplate furnished with the Nova Comet lathe; aluminium faceplate with steel insert supplied with the Nova DVR 3000 lathe; manufactured faceplate using a washer with a nut welded to it.

Important points about faceplates:

- Faceplates come in diameters from 2in (50mm) for the mini-lathes and up to 8in (approx. 200mm) or more for the larger lathes, which are capable of handling very large, heavy chunks of wood. The larger or longer the piece of wood, the greater the number of screws that are required to hold the wood onto the faceplate. Generally, four screws is the minimum number of holes in the faceplate and, on many faceplates, the holes are sized to accept a No. 12 wood screw.

Never use drywall screws to mount faceplates to the wood, because they are fairly brittle and can break without warning.

- A faceplate works best – and holds the wood most securely – when it is mounted to a very flat surface, so that the entire surface of the faceplate mates with the wood. On mill-sawn pieces this is fairly simple; however, when working with chainsaw-cut wood, the surface is seldom smooth and perfect. If the faceplate is less than 3in (75mm), I recommend the purchase of a 3in (75mm) diameter Forstner bit that can be mounted in a drill press to cut a flat surface for the faceplate.

- If the faceplate is larger, mount the wood between centres, with the part to be mounted on the faceplate at the tailstock end, then turn a flat area for the faceplate. Since the faceplate will generally have a hole in the centre, size a tenon on the part supported by the tailstock that will just slip into the faceplate hole, as this will help to provide centring of the wood onto the faceplate. This flat surface is best cut with a fingernail-ground bowl gouge used in a shear-scraping mode. The cutting should be done from near the centre towards the outside. Check for flatness with a straightedge, or the side of the tool.

Fig 1.12 **The John Reed System consists of a threaded hub that screws onto the lathe spindle, and one or more threaded disks that will screw onto the threaded end of the hub. The advantage of this system is that you can have a large number of faceplates at a reasonable cost. It is especially useful in the school environment where a student may wish to keep their project ready to remount on the lathe for some period of time.**

The John Reed Faceplate

John Reed developed a faceplate system that is worthy of mention. This consists of a hub that screws onto the lathe spindle and then a number of plates that screw onto the hub. This system allows the turner to own a number of faceplates that may be left attached to a rough-turned bowl or vessel while it is drying before final turning. Thus, the remounting of the workpiece is simplified. The plate is simply screwed back onto the hub (see Fig 1.12, left).

Making a Faceplate

Good-quality faceplates can be expensive. Because of this, many people choose to make their own, as this allows a larger number of faceplates on hand for about the same amount of money as a single, purchased faceplate. Some years ago, when I had several lathes with ¾in x 16 tpi spindles, this is the method I used to make up some 2in (50mm) faceplates for them:

1 Mount an unhardened nut of the appropriate size on the spindle, with several washers to shim the nut out from the spindle; cut a recess in the threaded section which is equal to the parallel unthreaded registration section of the spindle.

2 Reverse the nut onto the lathe spindle and tighten it so that the back surface of the nut is firmly mated with the spindle flange surface.

3 Use an HSS parting tool to turn a spigot on the top of the nut that is a very tight fit to the hole that is the inside of a 2in (50mm) washer. If the turned-down part does not quite enter the hole in the washer, place the washer flat-side down on the anvil, align the tenon on the nut with the hole, place a chunk of hardwood on top of the nut, and drive the tenon into the washer with a heavy hammer. Weld the washer to the nut.

4 After welding in place, drill four holes around the washer; these will be the fixing holes for the screws.

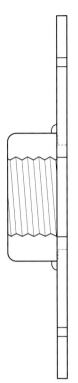

Fig 1.13 **This is how the faceplate will look, once assembled and welded**

Warning

Use unhardened and uncoated washers and nuts. Plated washers and nuts will not weld properly, and you will not be able to turn hardened nuts.

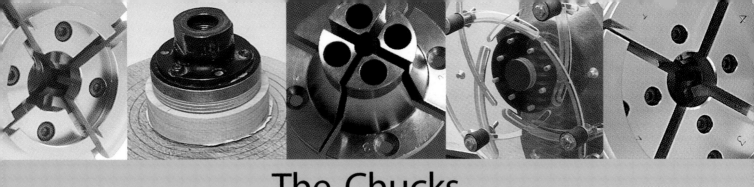

The Chucks

2 The Jam Fit Chuck

The jam fit chuck is the least expensive work-holding chuck available. It does not even require a faceplate or other screw-on attachments: it simply requires the turning of a piece of scrap wood to fit into the Morse taper in the headstock spindle. When you cannot think how to hold a workpiece on the lathe, and wish you had a chuck, just remember that you do have one, as close as the scrap box.

Jam fit chucks – which rely on a friction grip to hold or drive the work – were used for many years before other forms of chucks were invented. Anything that has been turned can be inserted into or onto a jam fit chuck; and actually, it doesn't have to be turned round: a round hole can be drilled into the workpiece and it can then be mounted onto a tenon turned on a jam fit chuck for turning.

There are two types of jam fit chuck, each of which may also have external or internal holding surfaces:

(1) The Jam Fit Chuck for Bowl or Box Turning

This is generally made from a piece of scrap wood and mounted onto a faceplate and has the grain running perpendicular to the axis of rotation of the lathe. There may be a recess in the face of the scrap wood, into which the outside edge of the bowl or box is pressed, or a short tenon over which the inside of the bowl or box is pressed. The fit must be snug enough to hold the workpiece on the lathe for turning of the surface facing outwards (or towards the tailstock), but not so snug that it will crack, or otherwise damage, the workpiece.

(2) The Jam Fit Chuck for Turning Small Workpieces

This type of jam fit chuck is mounted with the wood grain in spindle mode, or so that the grain is parallel to the axis of rotation of the lathe. It may also have a recess for the workpiece to be pressed into, or a tenon for the workpiece to be pressed over. This chuck is sometimes simply used as a friction drive, with the tailstock brought up for support on longer workpieces.

Jam fit chucks of this type are generally made of high-quality, close-grained woods such as boxwood, hard maple, or other dense woods. They can also be made from more sturdy materials, such as metal, when a large number of a single product is being produced. These chucks may be mounted onto a faceplate or, specifically for jam fit chucks that will be retained for repeated use, may have threads to fit the lathe spindle cut into the base of the chuck, or the mounting end turned into a Morse taper to fit the lathe spindle.

Jam Fit Chuck with External Grip

The jam fit chuck with external grip works the same, regardless of how the wood is oriented. However, for best results, the grain orientation used with the jam fit chuck should match the grain orientation of the workpiece. The sides of the recess must press onto the outer surface of the workpiece with enough pressure to hold it into the recess while the lathe operator is cutting away wood from the workpiece, and it must do so without damaging the workpiece. In addition, it must have a completely flat surface to engage the workpiece, so that it will run true after installation into the chuck (see Fig 2.1, right).

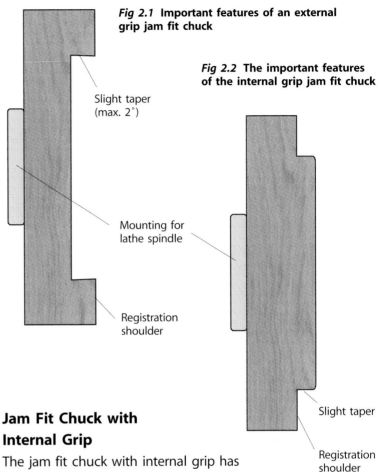

Fig 2.1 Important features of an external grip jam fit chuck

Slight taper (max. 2°)

Fig 2.2 The important features of the internal grip jam fit chuck

Mounting for lathe spindle

Registration shoulder

Slight taper

Registration shoulder

Note that the surface entering the chuck must bottom in the recess if that part has been turned true with the rest of the workpiece. If that part of the workpiece has not been turned true, then a shoulder must be provided that is turned true. This shoulder might be the bottom of a bowl when the foot is inserted into the recess, or an actual shoulder, as in the case of a box. If the top of a bowl is being inserted into a recess, then the top rim must bottom into the recess for the bowl to run true.

Jam Fit Chuck with Internal Grip

The jam fit chuck with internal grip has a tenon that must fit into a recess on the workpiece, i.e. into the mouth of the bowl or box. This chuck must have a true surface for the rim of the bowl or box to contact, and this surface must be turned smooth and flat to ensure the workpiece will run true (see Fig 2.2, above right).

The jam fit chuck with internal grip should have a shoulder at the base of the tenon that is turned true for the workpiece to mount against. It is not advisable to use the end of the tenon for this purpose.

Why Use a Jam Fit Chuck?

People who do not own another form of chuck can use this inexpensive alternative to enable them to turn more difficult tasks. For example, you could start a bowl between centres:

1 Turn the external shape completely, including a foot for the bowl (this can be the tenon to use in the jam fit chuck).

2 Mount a piece of scrap wood onto a faceplate and cut a jam-fit recess into the face of the scrap wood.

3 Make sure that the surface of the scrap wood runs true, then mount the bowl into the jam fit chuck. The bottom side of the bowl should mate with the front surface of the jam fit chuck.

I have turned many bowls in this manner when I have wanted a size for the bowl foot that did not fit any of my chucks.

After the inside of the bowl has been turned, sanded, and finished, pop the bowl out of the chuck and make another jam fit chuck to accept the rim of the bowl. This is used to hold the bowl to clean up, or turn away, the foot. It may be wise to fit it a bit less snugly into this second jam fit chuck and to use the tailstock to hold the bowl in the recess.

When this is done, place a small piece of wood between the bowl bottom and the point of the rotating centre. When you have finished turning, use a chisel to carve away the little column supporting the tailstock and then remove all traces of it with sandpaper.

Using the Jam Fit Chuck for Boxes

I have described the most common uses of a jam fit chuck for turning bowls, but there are other projects besides bowls, and many of these cannot be held properly in jam chucks, or by other means. Over the years I have made many boxes in the following manner, with a jam fit chuck mounted on a faceplate to hold the pieces for turning:

1 Turn the stock round and to a desired diameter on the normal drive centres of the lathe, then part the lid from the body of the box.

2 Make a jam fit chuck to hold the lid for hollowing. This jam fit chuck must have a hole in the centre, so that a dowel can be inserted to push the work out if it gets stuck in the recess. Hollow the lid, turn the face true, then set aside.

3 Mount the body of the box into the chuck and true up the face.

4 Hollow the box, making sure that enough material is left for a tenon to fit into the lid, then turn the tenon to fit the lid very snugly.

5 Use this tenon as the jam fit chuck to turn the outside and top of the lid, and turn the outside of the body of the box to final shape.

6 Sand the outside, apply a finish, then remove the lid and sand – or lightly turn – the tenon on the box, so that the lid fits with the desired snugness.

The box is then ready for a final jam fit chuck. This time the chuck can have a tenon to extend into the mouth of the box, or a recess to mate with the tenon that fits into the lid. Either method will give good results if the inside of the box is straight. If the inside walls of the box are not straight, then a recess to accept the tenon for the lid must be used. When the body of the box is mounted and running true, the bottom of the box may be finished.

When to Use a Jam Fit Chuck

I own a goodly number of chucks, each fitted with different types and sizes of jaws to meet many different holding needs, yet I often use the jam fit chuck because it is easy to make and generally does less damage to the workpiece than a shop-bought metal chuck would. Besides, there seem to be a narrow range of sizes that will not fit any of my chuck jaws. The alternative then is to turn the tenon smaller or the recess larger to fit one of the chucks, or to make a jam fit chuck. I often choose the latter option.

How to Make a Jam Fit Chuck

As discussed previously, there are four basic types of jam fit chuck: two of them on faceplate-mounted wood with the grain running perpendicular to the axis of rotation of the lathe, and two of them with the grain running parallel to the axis of rotation of the lathe. The same basic procedure works for making each of these types. The chuck described here uses wood mounted on the faceplate with the grain running perpendicular to the axis of

rotation of the lathe, and assumes that the workpiece is a bowl:

1 Mount on the faceplate a piece of scrap wood that is at least 1½in (38mm) thick and of adequate diameter when rounded to handle the workpiece.

2 To prevent marring the surface of the bowl, use scrap wood that is softer than the wood you are using for the bowl; I often use pine or fir scrap wood, but alder and other softer hardwoods would work equally well. The wood for the jam fit chuck must be dry, to remain as stable as possible.

Never leave the workpiece mounted on the jam fit chuck for any period of time. Even overnight may be too long. The changes in ambient moisture level can cause the woods to change in size and may cause your workpiece to dislodge from the chuck.

3 Mount the bowl blank between centres and turn and finish the outside, including a suitable foot for mounting into the jam fit chuck. Turn the foot with its sides almost parallel, but slightly tapered (maybe ½°) from the bottom of the foot to the base of bowl. This taper is very small, but is necessary to allow the foot to enter the jam fit chuck and make complete contact with the sides of the chuck recess, which also must be tapered slightly with the greatest diameter at the top of the recess.

The depth of the recess must allow the foot of the bowl to enter until the bottom of the bowl can make contact with the top of the jam fit chuck. I've said this before, but it is so important to the success of the project that I must repeat it.

4 Once the scrap wood has been mounted on the chuck, turn it true and flat.

5 Set a pair of dividers to the diameter of the very bottom of the foot of the bowl (which will be less than that at the base of the bowl proper).

6 With the lathe rotating, set both points of the dividers on the toolrest and adjust until it appears centred. Then, touch the left point to the rotating wood. Make sure the right point never touches the rotating wood, or it will catch and be carried up and around to slam down on the toolrest and may damage your bowl, your dividers, or yourself.

This is very important and worth repeating again and again:
the right point of the dividers must not touch the rotating wood!

7 The point of the dividers will scribe a circle on the face of the waste block. Stop the lathe and check the diameter of the circle with the dividers – if the circle is exact, you are ready to start hollowing the recess for the bowl foot. If the circle is larger than desired, turn away the surface to get rid of the circle and try again. If it is smaller, then make another circle that is slightly larger than the existing one. Repeat this until the diameter is right.

8 Next, repeat this operation with the dividers set to the diameter at the top of the foot (the part that joins the remainder of the bowl). This will give you two circles on the face of the waste block, one for the smallest diameter of the foot and one for the largest diameter of the foot.

9 Drill a hole in the centre of the block – at least the depth of the foot of the bowl – using a spindle gouge or drill.

10 Make a hollow by cutting towards the centres of the recess into this hole. Work back towards the inside scribed line using a gouge, if you like, until you are getting close to the line.

11 At this point, I recommend the use of a small, square-nose scraper, or a sharp skew chisel lying on its side in scrapermode, with the long point doing the cutting to cut the wall of the recess. If you cut this recess straight down, you will now have a hole with straight sides that the bottom of the bowl foot will just enter. Check the fit now.

12 If the foot just barely enters the recess, use your scraper or skew to cut a tapered wall from the outside circle to the bottom of the recess, creating a recess that the foot of the bowl just fits into with some pressure. I actually like to have this recess so snug that it requires a small mallet to drive the foot of the bowl into the recess, until the bottom of the bowl touches the face of the waste block.

In the event that the foot of the bowl simply presses into the recess, all is not lost. If the amount of oversize is small, applying moisture to the foot of the bowl and to the recess can cause the wood to swell enough to tighten the fit and make it work. If that doesn't work, don't give up, try using a thickness of paper towel to take up the slack. If you also dampen the towel or the recess, the hold will often be very satisfactory. If neither of these ploys work, turn away a little of the face of the waste block and slightly deepen the recess. Since the hole was tapered, the hole will now be smaller. This takes a little practice, but is really quite easy.

13 Make sure that the base of the bowl touches all of the way around, then bring up the tailstock and turn on the lathe to check if the bowl runs true. If so, you're ready to go. Otherwise, stop the lathe and place the toolrest close to the top edge of the bowl and check for high and low points. Tap with the mallet on the high points. Continue this until there is no visible change as you rotate the lathe. Again, turn on the lathe and check that the bowl is running true.

14 Keeping the tailstock in place to give the jam fit chuck as much support as possible (see Fig 2.3), hollow the bowl, except for the small column at the very centres, where the tailstock is providing support.

Fig 2.3 **Supporting the jam fit chuck with the tailstock**

15 Once the bowl is to depth, you should be able to back off the tailstock and remove the centres column. Sand and finish the inside of the bowl, and you are almost done.

16 To refine the foot of the bowl, make a jam fit chuck that will hold the rim of the bowl while the foot is turned. Since the bowl wall is now fairly thin, do not make this fit a drive fit, but rather a press fit.

17 Bring the tailstock up with a small piece of wood between the bottom of the foot and the point of the tail centres to protect the bottom of the foot.

18 Turn the foot, except for that little column in the centres, which can be removed off the lathe, with a chisel and some sandpaper. Alternatively, use Duct tape or 'gaffer' tape to hold the bowl into the jam fit chuck, for that little bit of turning to remove the small column of wood from the tail centres. If the jam fit chuck fits well enough, the tape can provide all of the support required during the final turning, sanding and finishing of the foot (see Fig 2.4, below).

Fig 2.4 **Using tape to help hold a bowl in a jam fit chuck while the bottom is turned**

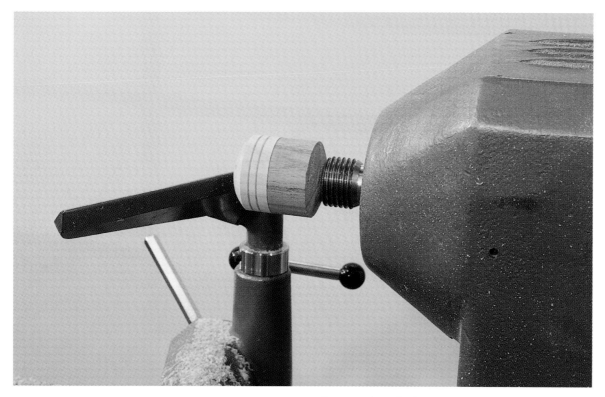

Fig 2.5 **A jam fit chuck held to the lathe spindle with a wooden Morse taper extension**

When making the opposite form of jam fit chuck, i.e. where the workpiece fits over a tenon on the chuck, the process is exactly the same as described above, except that the workpiece is the part with the recess, and the chuck is the part that fits into the recess. This type of chuck can be used for turning the bottoms of boxes, turning rings, and turning items such as thimbles (see Fig 2.5, above).

3 The Glue Chuck

Glue may be used in various ways to mount and hold wood on the lathe for turning. The glues discussed here are the cyanoacrylate (CA) glues, the yellow glues such as Titebond II – an aliphatic resin– and hot-melt glue. I also discuss the use of another sticky substance, double-backed tape, to mount work for turning.

The glue chuck is only slightly more expensive than the jam fit chuck discussed in Chapter 2. In fact, a loose-fitting jam fit chuck may easily be turned into a glue chuck by the simple addition of glue to hold the workpiece more securely in the chuck. As with the jam fit chuck, the basic glue chuck is a faceplate with a waste block mounted to its surface. The waste block must be turned true with the axis of rotation

of the lathe. It should be noted, however, that it is not even necessary to have a faceplate for smaller pieces.

An adequate glue chuck may be made by first turning a Morse taper on the end of a spindle and leaving a larger surface on the other end – turned true to the axis of rotation – to attach the workpiece with glue (see Fig 3.1, below). A glue chuck can be used over and over again, as can a jam fit chuck, but eventually the waste block will require replacement, as its surface approaches the ends of the mounting screws. Many bowl turners use the glue chuck exclusively to turn their bowls.

Methods of Glue Chucking

Paper Insert
Perhaps the most common method of glue chucking is the use of a paper insert. For this method, the glue is applied on both the surface of a glue block mounted on the faceplate, and on the bowl blank. A piece of sturdy paper is then placed between the two pieces as they are joined. The paper must be sufficiently sturdy to prevent the glue bleeding through the paper, or the purpose of the paper is defeated. I found that brown paper grocery bags worked pretty well.

The paper insert is considered by some to be a very good and inexpensive way to mount bowl blanks onto the lathe; generally, for this

Fig 3.1 A Morse taper glue chuck for holding very small items

Fig 3.2 **This shows the assembly of a paper-insert glue chuck. The paper must be heavy enough to prevent the glue from soaking completely through, otherwise the paper may not separate when it is time to remove the workpiece from the glue chuck.**

form of mounting, the entire bowl is turned inside and out, sanded, finish applied, then a sharp chisel used to split the paper and remove the bowl from the waste block. At this point, the paper and glue are sanded away from the foot, and finish applied. The bowl is turned with only one mounting, unless you wish to have the foot look as if it has also been turned, in which case a jam fit chuck is used to reverse the bowl, so that the foot can be turned and decorations added.

Although I've never had a paper joint fail, I have never felt too secure with one either, and I am not a fan of this form of mounting. I've also heard of other woodturners having the paper glue joint break with a catch. However, when I did use it, this is the method I used to mount the turning block to the faceplate-mounted waste block:

1 Mount the waste block to the faceplate with sheet-metal screws and attach the faceplate to the lathe spindle.

2 Turn the waste block round, and the surface of it smooth and perpendicular to the axis of rotation.

3 Find and mark the centre of the turning blank. If it is square, you can do this very effectively with a straightedge aligned with two opposing diagonal corners of the bowl blank. Repeat for the second set of corners. The cross of these two lines designates the centre of the bowl blank.

4 Using a compass or dividers, draw a circle – or a series of circles – centred on the bowl blank that matches the diameter of the waste block. You will use this circle to centre the waste block onto the bowl blank.

5 With the compass setting matching the diameter of the waste block, draw a circle on the paper insert and cut out this circle of paper.

6 Apply Titebond or Titebond II glue to both the waste-block face, and to the area inside the circle on the bowl blank which is to be used to centre the waste block. Other glues may well work just as well, but I've long been a fan of Titebond II glue for gluing wood.

7 Lay the paper disk onto the circle drawn on the bowl blank.

8 Centre the waste block and faceplate onto the paper disk and apply pressure, using clamps or a suitable weight.

9 Wipe off excessive glue and allow to dry overnight.

10 Mount the faceplate with the attached bowl blank onto the lathe, and turn your bowl.

Bowl Blank Glued Directly onto the Waste Block

The method of glue chuck that I have always favoured is to glue the bowl blank directly to the waste block. I believe that gluing directly provides a much more secure mounting and I've turned a good number of bowls and other items with this mounting. This method can be used with different types of turning and is not limited to turning bowls. Basically, the process of mounting bowl blanks is the same as for the paper insert glue chuck, you simply leave out the paper insert (see Fig 3.3, below).

If you are using this type of mounting for something other than a bowl blank – such as a goblet – I recommend turning a slight recess in the waste block to receive the end of the turning blank, which will greatly simplify the centring of the turning blank onto the waste block. Many people use concentric circles to align the turning blank to the centre of the waste block, but I've found that a 1/16in (2mm) recess is much more positive than a pencil-drawn circle.

For this type of mounting, medium-thick CA glue will work very well: apply the glue to one surface, then briefly apply the other surface to the glued one, so that the glue is transferred to that surface as well. Separate, apply accelerator to one of the surfaces, then stick them together. They will be ready to turn in a couple of minutes.

Fig 3.3 **Here the bowl blank is glued directly to the wood waste block mounted on the faceplate. This is a much more positive form of mounting than the paper insert mounting.**

I do not recommend CA glue for mounting bowl blanks – although some people do use it – because it tends to become brittle and a sudden jolt like a heavy catch may break the glue joint, resulting in an airborne bowl.

Using Hot-melt Glue

Hot-melt glue can also be used to glue the workpiece to the waste block. I've used this method a number of times when I didn't have a set of chuck jaws to match the size of foot on a bowl; I started the bowl and turned the outside and a foot with the bowl blank held between centres, mounted on a screw chuck, or on a faceplate. I then mounted the foot of the bowl onto a waste block with hot-melt glue, but this does require some means of centring the bowl blank onto the waste block very precisely.

I saw Vic Wood of Australia demonstrate the following method, using hot-melt glue:

1 Place a spindle thread mounted on a Morse taper into the tailstock Morse taper, then screw the faceplate onto the threads at the tailstock.

2 Place a faceplate with a waste block onto the lathe spindle, then simply bring the tailstock up with the mounted bowl, and align the foot of the bowl and the waste block perfectly.

Fig 3.4 **A method of mounting a bowl blank onto a waste block with hot-melt glue**

3 Apply hot-melt glue to the foot of the bowl, press it against the waste block and, for added support, run a bead of hot-melt glue around the seam between the bowl blank and the waste block.

4 Once the inside of the bowl is turned, heat the glue joint (heat from a hairdryer works fairly well) and pull it apart.

Hot-melt glue has never been one of my favourite methods of work-holding, but it is quick (see Fig 3.4, below).

Methods of Centring Work on a Glue Chuck

In the case of small work, such as goblets and tops, one can make concentric circles on the waste block, or cut a shallow recess in the

Fig 3.5a & b **Centring a workpiece on the waste block for a glue chuck mounting, using a little tenon on the foot of the bowl blank**

easily to a glue chuck, by turning a recess in the face of the waste block that will accept the little tenon in the centre of the foot of the bowl. This provides a very positive centring of the bowl blank to the waste block and it also works very well on other items started between centres (see Fig 3.5a & b).

Using Double-backed Tape

waste block to accept the workpiece. For bowl blanks, the concentric circles must be drawn on the bowl blank, and the waste block mounted on a faceplate aligned by the circles. It is not practical to have a waste block large enough to cut a recess in it to align the bowl blank. Figs 3.2 through 3.4 (on pp. 35–7) show the application of the waste block to a bowl blank using concentric circles for centring.

The workpiece may be started between centres and then transferred to a glue chuck for final turning. This is quite common for goblets, vases, and so on, and is not uncommon for bowls. It is fairly easy to start a bowl between centres, turn the complete outside including a foot, and leave the centre point on a small tenon that extends from the centre of the foot of the bowl. Although I now normally mount the bowl foot in a four-jaw scroll chuck to final-turn the bowl and hollow the inside, I can also mount this bowl

Carpet tape should never be used, as it tends to release suddenly; the tape designed for mounting pieces for woodturning – industrial strength double-backed tape – seems to let go slowly when it starts to fail, and this allows you to detect the problem and shut down the lathe before the piece becomes airborne. When using double-backed tape, occasionally check the mounting of the workpiece to ensure that the tape is still holding firmly. A cut that seems wrong may be an indication that the double-backed tape is beginning to fail.

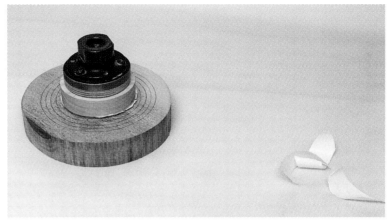

Fig 3.6a & b **Using double-backed tape to mount a bowl blank to a waste block**

The use of double-backed tape is very similar to the use of a paper-insert glue chuck:

1 Stick the double-backed tape to a waste block, or directly to the surface of the faceplate. Since this tape is not wide, it will take several strips to cover the faceplate. Trim off excess tape from around the edge of the faceplate.

2 Your faceplate must run true; if yours doesn't, mount a waste block to the faceplate and true the face of the waste block.

3 Apply the tape to the waste block, pull off the protective strip from the topside of the tape, and you have a very sticky surface ready to receive your workpiece.

4 Centre the workpiece onto the faceplate and apply pressure for at least 15 minutes. When the combined faceplate and workpiece is small enough, clamp it into a vice. Alternatively, use several clamps – or a heavy weight – to apply pressure.

Never leave a bowl blank that has been mounted with double-backed tape on the lathe, or you may return to find your partially finished bowl lying on the floor, because the tape does not stand up well to downward pressure, which pulls the workpiece away from its mounting.

When you are finished turning a workpiece mounted with double-backed tape, simply apply pressure from one side, pulling outward in a sort of arc. After a bit, the tape will begin to separate; continue to apply pressure until the workpiece is free. Alternatively, you could slip a thin, sharp chisel into the joint of tape and workpiece and apply a tipping pressure to break the seal, but this requires care to avoid damaging your workpiece.

4 The Screw Chuck

The screw chuck is simply a faceplate with a single, large screw mounted in the centre, so that a workpiece may be screwed onto it quickly and removed again quickly as the need arises. The wood to be turned must have a hole drilled into it that is a little smaller than the core diameter screw. There are a large number of screw chucks available. Many of the four-jaw scroll chucks are supplied with a large screw; this can be grasped by the chuck, thus making the four-jaw chuck into a screw chuck also (see Fig 4.1).

One of the most common uses for a screw chuck is holding the wood to turn the outside of a bowl blank. It can be used to hold virtually any piece of wood for turning, but it is best when screwed into the wood plank-wise – the screw doesn't hold as well when screwed into endgrain. Many people use a screw chuck to hold the waste block for a jam fit chuck. It is also often used to hold the waste block for a glue chuck. Soren Berger, a New Zealand woodturner, says that he uses the screw chuck to hold bottle-

Fig 4.1 **The different components of a screw chuck**

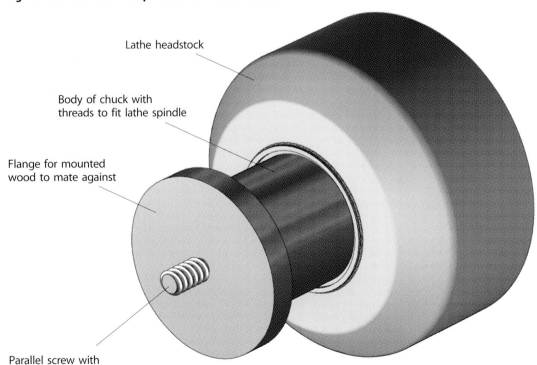

Lathe headstock

Body of chuck with threads to fit lathe spindle

Flange for mounted wood to mate against

Parallel screw with sharpened threads

stopper knobs while turning. This is screwing into the endgrain, but on such a small turning that it apparently works quite well.

For many years, I have used the screw chuck to begin turning a bowl blank. My screw chuck has a 3in (75mm) faceplate to rest against the wood. Since most of my wood is not sawn plank-wise, but simply half of a log, I've used a 3in (75mm) Forstner drill bit to flatten an area for the faceplate of the screw chuck to butt against. This is a very important point when using the screw chuck: its faceplate must be able to butt smoothly against the wood for the most stable operation.

It is difficult to rotate the chunk of wood to screw it onto a screw chuck, so it is best to rotate the headstock spindle while the wood is held against the screw. This is fairly easy if your lathe has a handwheel, but not all lathes have one. I've found it works reasonably well to hold the hole in the wood against the screw and bring up the tailstock to press the wood against the screw; you can then rotate the wood while cranking in the tailstock to take up the slack. This works especially well when the wood is fairly heavy and hard (see Fig 4.2, below).

I once broke the screw on my screw chuck, because I did not make the surface smooth and flat for the faceplate to butt against – the faceplate was only touching about halfway around – and the torque applied as I turned the wood caused the screw to break. So, make sure that you have a flat surface and that the hole drilled for the screw is perpendicular to that flat surface. The Forstner drill is good for making a flat spot and it also makes an indentation to guide the drill to make the hole for the screw. Hence, the drilled hole is exactly in the centre of the 3in (75mm) flat spot and, if the wood is kept shimmed in the same way that it was when making the flat spot with the Forstner bit, the drill press should drill a hole perpendicular to the flat spot.

Fig 4.2 **Using the tailstock to help start the wood onto the screw chuck**

I've seen Richard Raffan hold the bowl blank in his hand and, with the lathe running, tipping the blank onto the screw and allowing the lathe to screw the blank on. Richard makes it look easy, but I can't recommend it for any beginning bowl turner. I first saw Richard do this at a symposium in 1992 and I still haven't had the nerve to try his method with the wood that I turn. I don't recall ever seeing another demonstrator use Richard's technique to mount the bowl blank. Most seem to screw them on by hand while the lathe is stopped, like I do.

The screw chuck doesn't work especially well on endgrain, since endgrain is cut by the screw and is often easily pulled out. The best way to use a screw chuck to hold a piece of endgrain wood is to glue a plank-wise piece of waste wood onto the bottom of the endgrain piece, so that the screw of the screw chuck is turning into wood that has some endgrain and some side grain. This allows the screw to hold quite well. Another possibility is to drill a hole through the workpiece and glue in a dowel so that, when the screw is screwed into the endgrain wood, it also encounters the side grain of the dowel, giving the screw much greater holding capability. Figure 4.3 illustrates the use of a waste block glued to the endgrain workpiece to provide better holding capability for the screw.

Fig 4.3 A waste block of plank-wise wood glued to the endgrain of a workpiece allows the screw chuck to have a more positive hold on the wood

The screw chuck is a fairly simple mounting and the chuck itself can be made up from a faceplate, a piece of scrap wood, and a large wood screw or lag screw. If making a home-made screw chuck, I recommend the use of a lag screw rather than a wood screw. The regular screw chuck screw is straight-sided, rather than tapered like a wood screw. Fig 4.4 shows how you can make up a simple screw chuck using a faceplate, a piece of scrap wood, and a lag screw as the holding device.

Fig 4.4 **A home-made screw chuck**

Making a Screw Chuck:

1 Mount a suitable piece of hardwood scrap to the faceplate.

2 Mount the faceplate on the lathe spindle, then turn the wood so that it is the same diameter as the faceplate.

3 While the faceplate is still on the lathe, place a Jacob's chuck into the Morse taper of the tailstock and drill a hole – of a slightly bigger diameter than the screw to be used – that will just allow the lag screw to pass through without hindrance.

4 Remove the faceplate from the lathe spindle, then insert the lag screw through the hole in the faceplate and through the hole in the waste wood.

5 Now screw the lag screw into a piece of wood – a bowl blank or any piece of hardwood – so that the screw can be tightened down firmly.

6 Apply epoxy around the head of the lag screw; this will help hold the screw in place when screwing on a workpiece, and prevent the lag screw rotating in the waste block as the workpiece is being turned.

I made up a few of these screw chucks before I finally purchased a good commercial screw chuck. Home-made screw chucks work reasonably well, but are never as good as the commercial units.

5 The Cup Chuck

Before the various movable jaw chucks became commercially available, the cup chuck was commonly used to hold wood on the lathe. In fact it is still used quite extensively in several parts of the world, including Japan and France and, I believe, by the small group of ornamental turners that practise this ancient form of turning.

The cup chuck is very similar to the jam fit chuck described in Chapter 2. The primary difference is that it is deeper and is designed for wood that is turned with the grain in spindle mode (grain parallel to the axis of

rotation). It is not as readily available on the market today, but it is still a very good form of chucking, especially for smaller items.

The cup chuck is a conical chuck, and is used to hold short pieces without the support of a tailstock. The workpiece is driven into the chuck with light blows, or by pressure exerted by the tailstock, and is one of the simplest of the early chucks developed for this purpose. The early cup chucks generally consisted of short metal cylinders that were bored or turned with a slight taper, not exceeding 2°. Originally, they were available in sizes from about ¼–6in (6–150mm) in diameter. Although they were made from metal, however, the turner sometimes prepared a special cup from a strong, close-grained hardwood such as boxwood (see Fig 5.1, left).

The wood to be inserted in the cup chuck was either carved – or turned between centres – to create a slightly tapered tenon to fit into the recess of the cup chuck. It was then pressed into the recess of the chuck with the tailstock, or driven into the chuck with a mallet.

Once the workpiece is mounted into a cup chuck, it must be tested to ensure that it is running true. There are many ways of doing this: an early method was to lightly touch the rotating workpiece with a piece of chalk, held firmly against the toolrest, and projecting just a little. If the wood was out

Fig 5.1 The various parts of a cup chuck

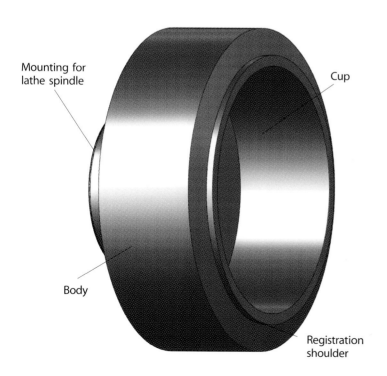

Mounting for
lathe spindle

Cup

Body

Registration
shoulder

of true, the chalk would touch the wood in the area that is out of true. The workpiece is then adjusted by gentle taps with a hammer to shift the wood in the chuck until it is correctly aligned.

It will take most hobby turners a while to adjust the cup-chuck-mounted workpiece to run true, but I have found that a tenon turned on the lathe, with a shoulder for the top of the cup chuck to butt against, almost always provides a workpiece that runs true.

I have always used from ½–1in (13–25mm) of tenon in my cup chucks to ensure proper holding. John Jacob Holtzapffel, in his book, *Hand or Simple Turning*, says, 'The hold that is afforded by an eighth of an inch of true contact, is generally found to suffice for work of any ordinary diameter.' This is probably true if the wood is dense and dry,

but in any chuck of this sort, it is not a good idea to leave the wood in the chuck for very long, say overnight.

Why Use a Cup Chuck?

With all of the modern chucks available on the market, why should you even consider using a cup chuck?

For one, it is inexpensive, especially if you make your own. Also, if you have a large number of identical pieces to make, you can turn the tenon for all of them between centres, then quickly press each of them into the cup chuck and start turning. You will note that I said 'press' them in. When the chuck is mounted on the spindle of your lathe, it is not a good idea to drive the wood into the cup chuck, as it would be hard on the bearings of the lathe, and heavy blows to wood being mounted into a cup chuck mounted on the lathe spindle should always be avoided. If you need heavy blows, remove the chuck from the spindle and place it on the floor or workbench.

I recently prepared the tenon on a piece of dry wood to fit into the cup chuck of my Escoulen ball and socket chuck a couple of weeks before a demonstration. We were going on vacation and returning a day or two before the symposium, so I did not re-check the tenon for fit. When I started work, the tenon had become a slip-fit into the chuck and I couldn't use it because it was too loose a fit. The wood must be a tight press-fit to work safely: if a partially turned piece is left in a cup chuck for some period of time with this sort of result, it might become airborne when the lathe is turned on.

Partially finished work cannot be removed from a cup chuck and remounted without some damage to the workpiece. Finish-turn the piece before removing it from the cup chuck.

If the workpiece fits snugly into the cup chuck, it may be difficult to remove it by knocking it out from the reverse side of the chuck, and the force required may damage the finished workpiece. The workpiece is normally removed from a cup chuck by parting off, and the waste wood is turned out of the cup chuck, or knocked out from the reverse side.

Combination Screw Chuck and Cup Chuck

Until recently, it was not uncommon for the workpiece to be pulled out of a cup chuck while turning and, once removed by an over-aggressive cut, it was nearly impossible to return the workpiece to the cup chuck so that it would run true. This has changed with a new sort of combination screw chuck and cup chuck which came on the market as I was starting this book. This 'die chuck', as it is called, is produced by Mortimers' Woodturning & Patternmaking in the United Kingdom. This is an interesting new product (see Fig 5.2, below) that fits roughly between the screw chuck of Chapter 4 and the cup chuck of this chapter. It provides more positive holding than a standard cup chuck, and may be useful for hollow-form turners as well as spindle turners. This chuck is described more fully in Chapter 12.

Although most of the cup chucks used in the past were made of metal for greatest strength and durability, many were also made from a good hard, dense wood such as boxwood. On the facing page I describe how to make a simple boxwood cup chuck that mounts into the No. 2 Morse taper of the lathe. Most of these will be for fairly small tenons, because it is difficult to obtain boxwood in large sizes (see Fig 5.3, opposite).

Fig 5.2 **The die chuck, which screws onto a tenon on the wood**

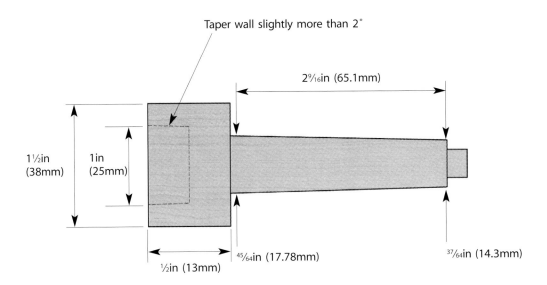

Taper wall slightly more than 2°

2⁹⁄₁₆in (65.1mm)

1½in (38mm)

1in (25mm)

45⁄₆₄in (17.78mm)

½in (13mm)

37⁄₆₄in (14.3mm)

Fig 5.3 **A dimensioned drawing of a home-made boxwood cup chuck**

Making a Simple Boxwood Cup Chuck

1 Use a piece of boxwood larger in diameter than the Morse taper of your lathe; this is essential, because a Morse taper must be cut on one end so that it can be mounted to the lathe spindle.

2 Mount the wood between centres (grain running parallel to the axis of rotation) and turn it to a smooth cylinder.

3 Lay out a section that will become the Morse taper part; this section should be 2¾in (67mm) long for a No. 2 Morse taper, which is the most common size for lathes in service today. The actual dimensions of a No. 2 Morse taper is 2⁹⁄₁₆in (65.1mm) in length with a small

diameter of 37⁄₆₄in (14.3mm) tapering to a large diameter of 45⁄₆₄in (17.5mm). I like to add about another ½in (13mm) beyond the end that will be of a smaller diameter, to provide a section for the knock-out bar to hit. This prevents damage to the small end of the Morse taper.

4 Set your calliper to 45⁄₆₄in (17.78mm) for the large diameter end of the laid-out Morse taper, and make a parting cut to that dimension.

5 Next, set your calliper to the smaller diameter value of 45⁄₆₄in (17.78mm) and make a parting cut 2⅝in (66mm) to the left of the first parting cut.

6 Use a skew chisel to make a tapered cut that runs from the thickest part of the Morse taper down to the smallest diameter. Stop short of completion of the taper, and use a 2⁹⁄₁₆in (65.1mm) piece of wood with sandpaper attached to finish it off, to ensure that the taper is true along its length.

7 Turn down the ½in (13mm) extension beyond the small end of the taper to about ⁷⁄₁₆in (11mm) in diameter, just slightly smaller than the small end of the Morse taper. A ⁷⁄₁₆in (11mm) wrench makes a nice calliper for sizing this part.

8 Now, cut an extension of the Morse taper at the large end. I recommend reducing about ⅛in (3mm) to ¼in (6mm) beyond the beginning of the Morse taper to at least ⁴⁵⁄₆₄in (17.78mm), so that the shoulder does not hit the end of the spindle and possibly keep the taper from holding firmly.

9 With the Morse taper finished, remove the piece from between centres, knock out the headstock centre, and insert the new Morse taper into the headstock Morse taper. Tap it in lightly to seat it.

10 Clean up the outside of the remaining wood to run true to the new mounting – this part should be at least 1in (25mm) long. True up the end of the piece, and mark the centre with the long point of the skew chisel laying on its side. This is used to provide a centre point to assist the drill to start on centre.

11 Mount a Jacobs chuck in the tailstock with a drill that is slightly less in diameter than your planned cup chuck recess. This size will be determined by the overall diameter of your piece of boxwood. Assuming the boxwood is 1½in (38mm) in diameter, this hole should be a maximum of 1in (25mm). Now, mount a 1in (25mm) drill and drill a hole into the planned chuck that is about ¾in (20mm) deep. Do not go deeper than ¾in if the chuck portion is only 1in (25mm) long.

12 A side-cutting tool can now be used to create a slight taper from the top edge to the bottom. Do not make this taper greater than about 2° – in fact 1° would, perhaps, be better. Round over the very top lip of the hole, to help start the wood into the chuck, and the boxwood cup chuck is ready for use.

Although an ancient form of chuck, the cup chuck is still very useful today. There are many applications, when turning short pieces of wood that have the grain running parallel to the axis of rotation, in which the cup chuck is appropriate. It is also inexpensive to make.

6 The Pin Chuck

Pin chucks were commonly used in the earlier days of woodturning and, although they are not as commercially available as they once were, they are still very useful for starting bowls, turning bottle-stopper knobs, and so on; they do not work exceptionally well on softer woods, however, as the pin can sink into the wood and remove the holding power against the torque applied by the turning tools.

Basically, a pin chuck consists of a section of round steel rod with a V-shaped recess cut along its length, so that a small pin of about the same length can be placed into the recess (see Fig 6.1, below). Some method must be provided for attaching this steel rod to the lathe headstock spindle: a Morse-taper

mounting, a chuck or collet, or a threaded section on the end of the rod, to fit the headstock spindle, are some common mountings.

The small pin will be flush with the circumference line of the steel rod when it is in the centre of the recess, as shown in

Fig 6.1 The basic pin chuck

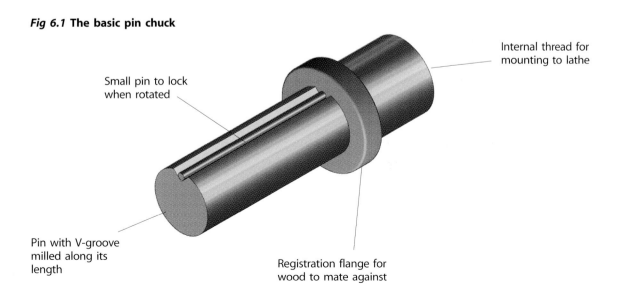

Small pin to lock when rotated

Internal thread for mounting to lathe

Pin with V-groove milled along its length

Registration flange for wood to mate against

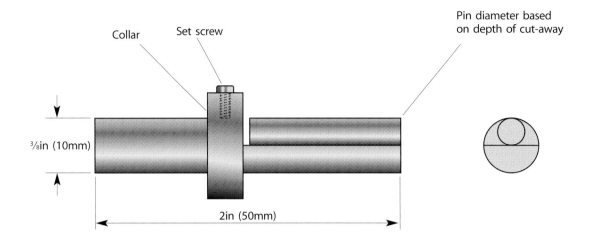

Collar   Set screw

Pin diameter based
on depth of cut-away

¾in (10mm)

2in (50mm)

Fig 6.2 **A simple pin chuck, for turning wine-bottle stoppers**

Fig 6.1 (previous page). When the rod – with the pin – is inserted into a hole drilled into a piece of wood that is a slip-fit for the rod, and the wood is rotated, the small pin shifts in the recess and jams against the wood; this stops the wood rotating while the lathe is running. When you are ready to remove the piece from the lathe, simply rotate the wood in the opposite direction to bring the small pin back to centre position and pull the wood from the round rod. Take care, as it is very easy to lose the small pin when the workpiece is removed.

I first encountered the pin chuck several years ago, when I purchased a new Record Power CL-3-48 lathe. The lathe came with a set of Record turning tools and a Record power chuck, which consisted of a number of pieces to handle different mounting conditions. The chuck was pretty frustrating to use, but I did like the 1in (25mm) pin chuck that was a part of the chuck system,

and I found it to be a good way to mount a bowl blank to turn the outside and foot of the bowl for chuck mounting. The 1in (25mm) diameter of the steel rod gave me more confidence than the ¾in (10mm) thread of my screw chuck. It was not quite as handy as a screw chuck, but the greater mass of the mounting made me feel a bit more secure when mounting larger bowl blanks. I did find that, if the wood was too soft (perhaps wet), the pin would simply embed itself into the wood, and the bowl blank would then rotate on the steel shaft from the force of cutting the wood. However, it did work very well with most woods suitable for turning.

When I first made bottle stoppers, I glued the ¾in (10mm) dowel into the stopper knob blank, holding the dowel with a dowel chuck (a Jacobs chuck that has had the jaws ground to fit snugly around a ¾in [10mm] dowel). I had a lot of dowel breakage with the harder woods and needed a metal dowel, or basically a small ⅜in (10mm) diameter pin chuck. At that time, I could not find one on the market and so made one from a piece of ⅜in (10mm) diameter steel rod, which could be held onto the lathe spindle with the dowel chuck; a flat about one third of the diameter of the rod deep, and about ¾in (20mm) long, was filed onto the end of the ¾in (10mm) steel rod protruding from the chuck. The pin was a piece of a nail – about one third of the diameter of the rod – that would fit onto the flat. That solved the problem – no more broken dowels.

It is now possible to buy these from Packard Woodworks in Tyron, North Carolina – I believe they have them in ⁵⁄₁₆in (8mm) and ⅜in (10mm) diameters. If you need a larger diameter pin chuck, it will be necessary to have a machine shop make one to suit your need.

Figure 6.2 (on facing page) shows the basics of a simple pin chuck for turning wine-bottle stoppers. If you are using regular corks, with a hole already drilled through to fit a particular size of dowel – in this case ⅜in (10mm) diameter – that is the size of steel rod that you will need. This rod must be long enough to be gripped by some sort of chuck or collet system, and provide ¾–1in (20–25mm) of extension to fit into the bottle-stopper knob blank. The pin chuck will also work best if there is a machined surface for the blank to mate against, to stop the blank from tipping. In the case of the first one that I made, there was no surface for the stopper blank to butt against, but the steel rod hitting the bottom of the hole seemed to do a fair job.

To Make the Pin Chuck Illustrated in Fig 6.2, You Will Need:

● A piece of brass or boxwood about ½in (13mm) long and about ¾in (19mm) in diameter to form a shoulder.

● A piece of steel rod of ⅜in (10mm) diameter (or whatever diameter of dowel needed to fit the commercial corks available) and about 2½in (62mm) long.

● A nail or a piece of small rod about ⅛in (3mm) in diameter, to make a good pin.

Method

1 Mount the brass or boxwood piece in a chuck on the lathe and drill the ⅜in (10mm) hole through its centre (or drill the hole with a drill press).

2 Mount the piece between centres and turn the outside and faces true to the centre hole.

3 Drill a small hole and tap to fit a set-screw of about ⅛in (3mm) in diameter. This is now a shaft collar, which could have been purchased from industrial suppliers. The commercial shaft collars measure about ¾in (20mm) in outside diameter and are about ⅜in (10mm) thick, a little smaller than the home-made collar described here. They would work quite well except that they are steel and can easily dull the tips of your tools as you cut down to size with the stopper blank.

4 Cut the ⅛in (3mm) diameter pin to about 1in (25mm) in length and bevel the ends slightly, by rotating them against a rotating grinding wheel.

5 File or grind the recess for the pin on one end of the ⅜in (10mm) rod. Grind the surface until the pin can be placed on the ground surface, and the collar just slips over the pin. This surface can be flat, if filed, or slightly concave, if ground, but the lowest point should be at the centre of the shaft.

6 Install the collar so that it is located 1in (25mm) from the end that was just ground to hold the pin, and tighten the set-screw to hold it in place. If wished, a little CA glue or epoxy can be placed under the collar to give additional support in use. The pin chuck is then ready to use.

7 Drill a ⅜in (10mm) hole slightly over 1in (25mm) deep in the bottle-stopper knob blank; either do this on a drill press, or by mounting the blank in a chuck and drilling the hole in the lathe. This latter method provides better centring of the hole and also allows you to true the face of the blank so that it is perpendicular to the axis or rotation.

8 Mount the pin chuck into a Jacobs chuck, ⅜in (10mm) collet chuck, or into small jaws on a four-jaw chuck – something to mount the pin chuck to run true on the lathe spindle.

Fig 6.3 **The home-made pin chuck in use, turning wine-bottle stoppers**

9 Lay the ⅛in (3mm) pin onto the flat that was ground onto the end of the chuck, then slip the stopper knob blank over the end of the chuck, pushing back until it touches the surface of the collar. It sometimes helps to bring up the tailstock, but it is not essential.

10 Switch on the lathe and turn the stopper blank to shape. If the tailstock with a live centre is used, it will be necessary to turn away the little dimple on the end when the tailstock is removed (see Fig 6.3, left).

Using this method to hold bottle-stopper blanks, the dowel for mounting the cork to the knob can be glued into the cork with less than 1in (25mm) protruding from the large end of the cork. When the stopper knob is turned, sanded and finished glue can be applied to the dowel and the face of the cork and then the knob can be slipped onto the dowel and the cork pressed against the knob. This process can provide a fairly easy production operation by drilling and facing off a number of knob blanks, gluing dowels into corks, turning the knobs on the pin chuck, and finally gluing the cork, dowel, and knob together to form the finished bottle stopper.

Larger pin chucks could be made in this manner, if held in a machinist three-jaw chuck or a woodturning four-jaw scroll chuck with jaws that would grip the diameter of rod being used. A commercial shaft collar could be purchased to provide a face for the workpiece to butt against, and a piece of ¼in (6mm) or ⅜in (10mm) round steel rod could be used for the pin. However, with the number of chucks with small jaws that will do the same task much more easily, the larger pin chucks are really a thing of the past: they are still usable for small-sized projects such as bottle stops and so on, but outdated for larger diameter works.

7 Machinist-type Moveable Jaw Chucks

The machinist chuck was developed to hold steel and other hard materials for turning. In the early 1800s, this type of chuck was referred to as a 'universal' chuck (see Fig 7.1, below), and was used to hold larger works. A form of the universal chuck, produced by Holtzapffel and Deyerlein for many years, used a scrolling mechanism to move all of the jaws simultaneously. They were generally available in a three-jaw chuck, in which all jaws moved in and out at one time, providing self-centring of the work. Today, machinist chucks are highly refined, and some are available with two jaws, three jaws, four jaws and even six jaws, but the three jaw seems to be the most popular for gripping cylindrical or concentric pieces.

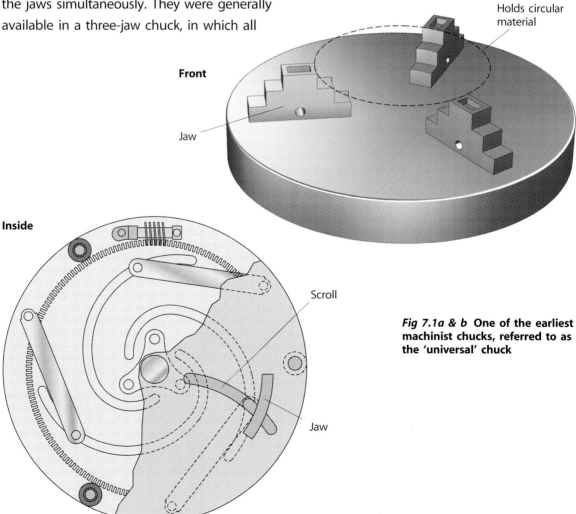

Front

Holds circular material

Jaw

Inside

Scroll

Jaw

Fig 7.1a & b **One of the earliest machinist chucks, referred to as the 'universal' chuck**

Fig 7.2 **A typical three-jaw machinist chuck**

The independent four-jaw chuck is used for very precise centring of the work; the three-jaw and four-jaw scroll chuck is not as precise as the independent four-jaw chuck, because wear and slop in the mechanism can introduce errors not acceptable in precision metal turning. Fig 7.2, above, shows a typical three-jaw chuck of this type, sold for use on woodturning lathes. The four-jaw chuck, in addition to providing a more precise set up, can also be used to grip odd-shaped pieces, to turn a part that is off-centre from the rest of the piece, or be used to produce eccentric works.

The machinist chuck was originally the only type of movable-jaw chuck available to woodturners. They did not work especially well, because the jaws were made to hold steel, brass and other hard materials, and they had a tendency to compress the wood fibres so that the jaws could not get the positive grip needed to hold the wood

properly. The jaws also compressed the wood more in some places than in others, so that the workpiece did not always run true when mounted in the chuck.

Although they do not hold normal turning woods well, they can be used effectively if the wood is very hard such as boxwood or African blackwood and they were often used by ivory and hardwood turners. They are not widely used today by woodturners, because of the advent of so many better methods of work-holding available – such as the four-jaw scroll chuck with jaws – which were developed specifically to hold wood. (These chucks are described at length in Chapter 9).

The machinist-type chuck generally has stepped jaws for gripping different sizes of work in a compression mode, and the jaws can often be removed and reversed if a step jaw configuration is not suitable. Fig 7.3 (overleaf) shows the same chuck with the jaws in normal mode and reversed.

They work equally well in expanding or contracting modes. The average machinist chuck is fairly large with 5in (127mm) diameter being on the minimal size and increasing in size from there.

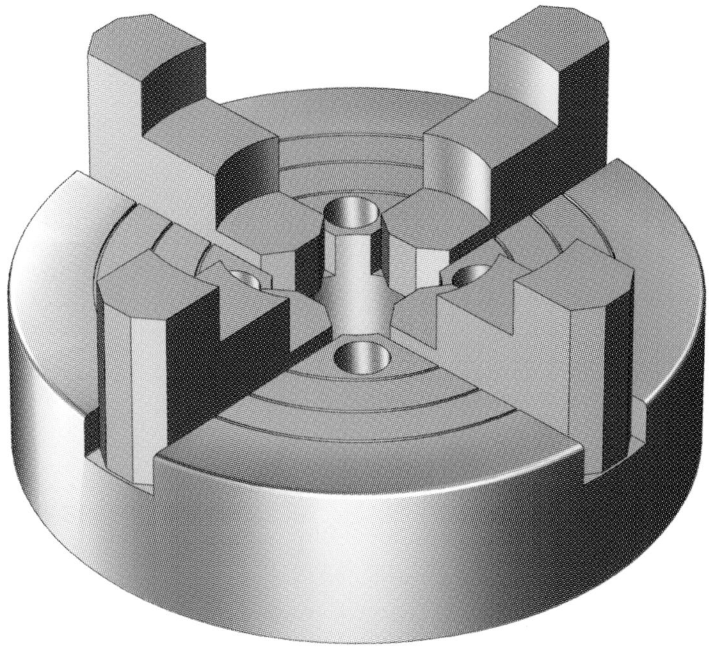

A number of companies sell small, machinist-type chucks as woodturning chucks, mostly for use on smaller wood lathes. Apart from the jaws not being designed to hold wood well, these chucks can be real knuckle-dusters, because the jaws often extend above the chuck body when expanded towards their maximum capacity. But for gripping dowels or woods that have already been turned round between centres, the three-jaw self-centring chucks can be quite useful in the woodturning workshop, and they are much less expensive than the four-jaw scroll chucks specifically designed for woodturning.

Fig 7.3a **(Above) Machinist four-jaw chuck with jaws in a normal mode, set to grip a large internal object or to grip different sizes of objects with an external grip. Each chuck jaw is independently adjustable for precise adjustment.**

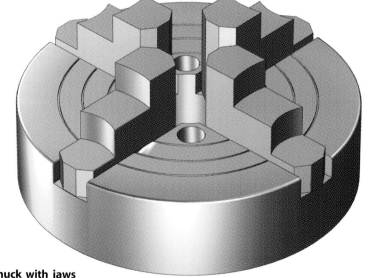

Fig 7.3b **(Right) Machinist four-jaw chuck with jaws in the reverse mode, and set for gripping smaller external objects on the outside, or various size pieces by expanding into a recess. Each chuck jaw is independently adjustable for precise adjustment.**

8 Jacobs Chucks and Collet Chucks

The Jacobs chuck and the collet chuck were designed for the metalworking trade, but are used extensively by woodturners, as they are extremely useful for holding smaller pieces.

Jacobs Chucks

The Jacobs chuck was made to hold drills for drilling metal and therefore has jaws that will easily bite into the surface of a piece of wood held by the jaws. However, when the jaws of the Jacobs chuck are ground to fit a specific size of material like the dowel chuck available from Craft Supplies USA in Provo, Utah, the chuck will provide excellent holding of woods of a specific size without damage to the work.

A. I. Jacobs invented the first three-jaw drill chuck and, in a way, this revolutionized the holding of drill bits. His company was founded in 1902 and still thrives today with a wide range of offerings. There are a lot of lookalike chucks on the market but, unless they have the register symbol in their name, they are not chucks from the Jacobs company; when I use the term 'Jacobs chuck', therefore, I am referring to the Jacobs-type chuck.

These chucks are available as key-operated chucks and as keyless chucks. For most woodturning applications, I like the keyed chuck. Figure 8.1 (above) shows

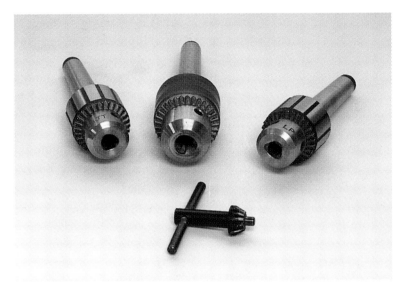

Fig 8.1 **A selection of Jacobs-type chucks used in the woodturning shop**

a number of different Jacobs-style chucks with No. 2 Morse taper mountings for use in either the headstock or the tailstock.

When used for woodturning, the Jacobs-type chucks are best used in the tailstock to hold drills and other objects made of metal, but they can also be used in the headstock to hold power buffs. When used to hold hardwood dowels they have a tendency to bite into the wood so that the dowel does not run true, but I know of a few people who use them to hold the dowel stem for spinner tops, and one who does this and turns out tops extremely fast, using a large Jacobs chuck and tightening it onto the dowel just with hand pressure – which keeps him from crushing the wood as readily.

This is because this size of chuck has larger flat areas on the jaws, so it is less likely to bite into the wood (see Fig 8.2, below).

The problem described for the Jacobs-type chuck is overcome with the dowel chuck sold by Craft Supplies USA; this is made up with ground jaws to mate with the outside of a ⅜in (10mm) dowel, which can grab and hold this size of dowel very tightly without damage to its surface. It was designed to hold the dowel for turning wine-bottle stoppers – a ⅜in (10mm) dowel glued into the stopper knob blank. I originally purchased one of these just for that purpose, but found it useful for a great many other applications as, by turning a ⅜in (10mm) diameter tenon on a piece of wood, one can turn a number of small items using this chuck.

I was turning bottle stoppers one day and noticed a pile of cut-off ends from spindle turnings; I realized that I could drill the centre of those cut-offs and glue in a ⅜in (10mm) dowel, and produce a spinner-top blank that used much less wood. Up to that time I had turned all of my spinner tops out of a square block of wood, as had everyone else I had seen turning them, but I could now turn several tops out of that block of wood with the use of some short pieces of dowel. Actually, the first ones were made with the same 2½in (62mm) lengths of dowel as I was using for my bottle stoppers – this length worked so well for the tops that I've continued to use it. Fig 8.3 (below) shows the Craft Supplies dowel chuck holding the ⅜in (10mm) dowel of a spinner top blank.

The dowel chuck can hold smaller-size dowels and tenons, but its best holding power and least damage to the wood occurs at exactly ⅜in (10mm) in diameter. This makes it very similar to a collet chuck, but it has a bit more flexibility.

Fig 8.2 **A wood tenon that has been gripped by a Jacobs chuck**

Fig 8.3 **The dowel chuck has the jaws ground to fit a ⅜in (10mm) diameter dowel**

Fig 8.4 **A selection of collets pulled into a No. 2 Morse taper**

The Collet Chuck

Unlike the Jacobs chuck, the collet chuck is designed to hold round objects of a specific size, and grips wood and steel equally without damaging the surface. It has excellent grip and causes minimal damage to one specific diameter of dowel or tenon. If it is designed for a ⅜in (10mm) tenon, that is the diameter that it will hold. You can't get a larger piece of wood into the collet and it will not close tightly on anything smaller than ⅜in (10mm), because the collet has a hole drilled or reamed to a specific size, a number of slits cut into the walls of the device, and is tapered on the outside; the collet is then pressed or pulled into a matching tapered recess, which bends the walls slightly to compress them onto the dowel. Figure 8.4 (above) shows a selection of collets that are pulled into the No. 2 Morse taper of the lathe spindle by a long threaded rod with a handwheel or wing nut at the back end of the spindle to pull the collet into the tapered hole of the spindle.

The Beall Collect Chuck

This collet chuck is designed to hold small parts very accurately without marring; it mounts to the lathe spindle and is available to fit a number of spindle sizes. It is of the compression type, so the collet is pressed into the recess by a screw-on cap. Because of the holding power of these precision-ground collets, spanners are not usually necessary and hand tightening will be sufficient for most wood work.

In addition to holding small wood pieces for turning, collet chucks are useful for holding mandrels, small shop-made faceplates, metal turning blanks and special jam chucks. Fig 8.5 (below) shows a Beall collet chuck.

Fig 8.5 **The Beall collet chuck compresses the collet into a tapered recess to tighten it onto a dowel or tenon**

Fig 8.6 **As shown here, collet chucks make a good holding base for turning spinning tops**

Fig 8.7 **Tool for removing bits of wood from the collet after parting off**

Advantages of the Collet Chuck

It evenly compresses the wood so that the dowel runs true; it has more room at the chucked end for manoeuvring of your turning tools; it holds extremely well; it is easy to release.

Disadvantages of the Collet Chuck

If you part-off your work close to the collet, you must have some way of removing the end of the dowel from the collet. Most collets of this type have a hole drilled into the collet for some distance. The dowel fits into the collet and bottoms against the end of the hole. Part-off close to the collet end and you have no way to grasp the waste wood to remove it from the collet. I have found that a drywall screw, with the head ground off and the shaft mounted into a wooden handle, makes an excellent tool for removing these pieces of waste wood (see Fig 8.7, above).

Modern Four-jaw Scroll Chucks

The modern four-jaw scroll chuck, designed for holding wood, is probably the chuck most widely used by woodturners today. These chucks use a scrolling mechanism to move the jaws in unison, and they hold equally well in compression or expansion mode. All are adaptations of an engineer's chuck.

I understand that the first purpose-built, woodturning four-jaw scroll chuck was the Nova chuck, made by Teknatool in New Zealand. There were many woodturning chucks on the market prior to the introduction of the Nova scroll chuck; depending on the make, these used various ways to move the jaws in unison, such as cones, rings or mandrels, and it was necessary to remove or add these in order to change from gripping in compression to expansion mode and vice versa. The Nova chuck used a scrolling mechanism and two levers to move the jaws for either expanding or contracting holding.

I purchased my first Nova chuck in the USA several years ago, when they first hit the market; soon afterwards close copies began to appear. Perhaps the Nova chuck technology was so similar to the machinist chuck that it could not be patented, otherwise these other makers could have been held at bay. Regardless, the chuck explosion has brought us woodturners a great number of new work-holding devices, and all these four-jaw scrolling chucks have a powerful grip, while being quick and easy to use.

> Four-jaw scrolling chucks are so powerful, in fact, that one must exert care or caution when tightening on the tenon of a bowl. Too much tightening – even from normal turning pressures – may help to shear off the foot. The same holds true when expanding into a recess – it is possible to exert so much pressure on some woods that the bowl splits during turning.

There are four main companies, in addition to Teknatool, that are producing these excellent four-jaw scroll chucks for woodturners: Oneway Manufacturing, Vicmarc, Axminster and Record Power with a recent addition. Because Teknatool's Nova chucks were first, and I have a great deal of experience with them, I will talk about them first.

The Nova Line of Chucks

The Basic Nova Chuck
The basic Nova chuck was the first of the four-jaw scrolling chucks built specifically for holding wood, and I find that it is a very

versatile unit. It is designed to offer a wide range of work-holding modes, combining the best features of present woodturning chucks with the advantages of engineering scroll chucks: wide jaw movement, quick action and powerful grip in either the contraction or expansion mode. The Nova also has some special features such as a travel stop on the jaw, and a unique action adjustment on the scroll movement (see Fig 9.1, below).

The basic Nova chuck comes equipped with a set of general-purpose 2in (50mm) dovetail/spigot jaws. These jaws are designed to expand into recesses, or contract around round/square wood spigots. Some irregular pieces can also be gripped. In both modes, any spigot or recess size can be selected between the minimum and maximum range of the jaws, but the greatest holding power in both expansion and contraction mode is

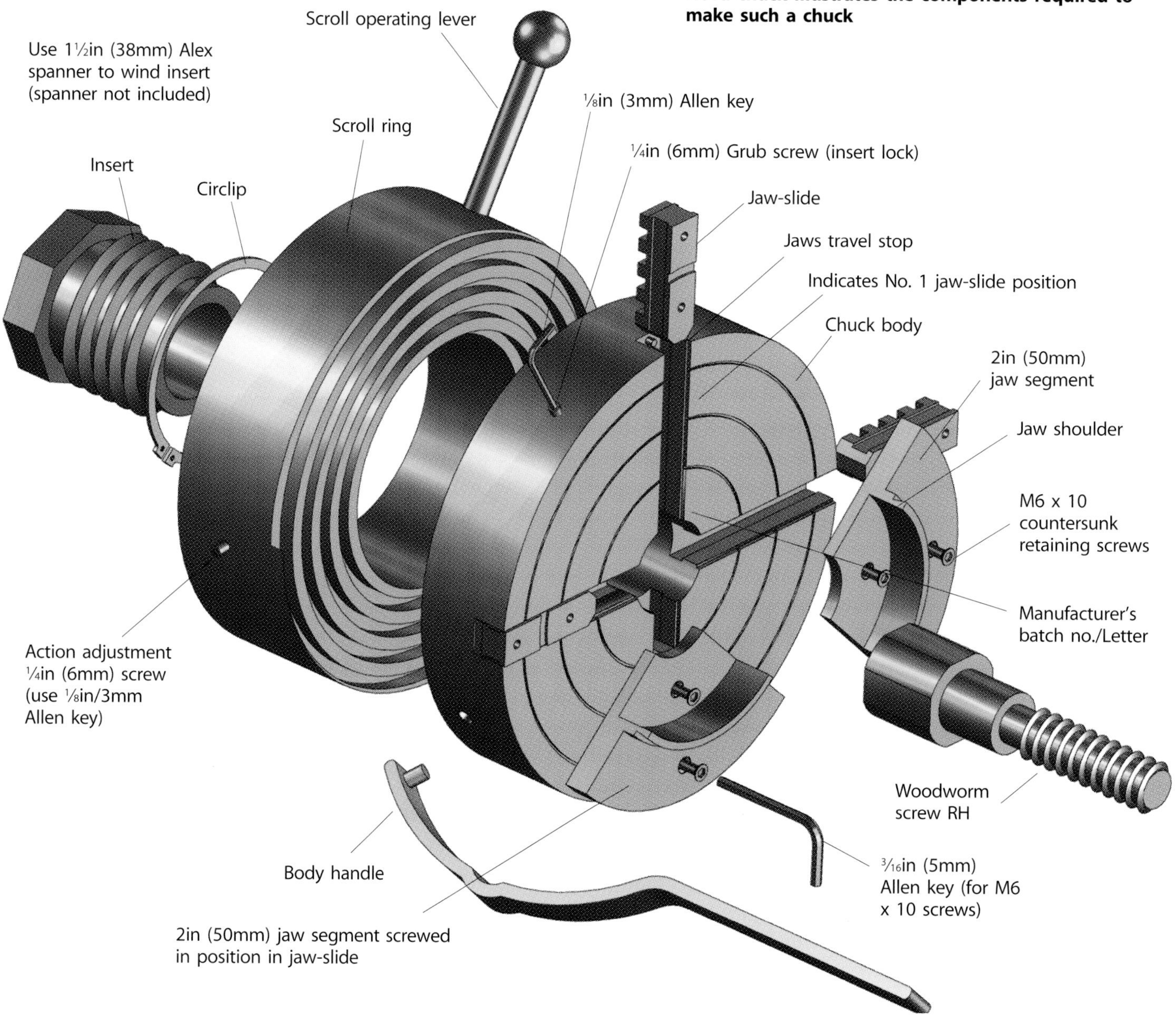

Fig 9.1 This exploded view of Teknatool's basic Nova chuck illustrates the components required to make such a chuck

Use 1½in (38mm) Alex spanner to wind insert (spanner not included)

Scroll operating lever

⅛in (3mm) Allen key

Scroll ring

¼in (6mm) Grub screw (insert lock)

Insert

Circlip

Jaw-slide

Jaws travel stop

Indicates No. 1 jaw-slide position

Chuck body

2in (50mm) jaw segment

Jaw shoulder

M6 x 10 countersunk retaining screws

Manufacturer's batch no./Letter

Action adjustment ¼in (6mm) screw (use ⅛in/3mm Allen key)

Woodworm screw RH

Body handle

³⁄₁₆in (5mm) Allen key (for M6 x 10 screws)

2in (50mm) jaw segment screwed in position in jaw-slide

when the jaws are set to grip a 2in (50mm) spigot; at that point, one obtains the greatest amount of surface contact between the chuck jaws and the wood (see Fig 9.2, right). The 2in (50mm) jaws can be removed to let the jaw-slides grip quite small spigots. The chuck is also supplied with a woodworm screw, which allows the chuck to function as a screw chuck.

The factory states that Nova chucks are 'sample-tested from each batch and are made to run within the following tolerance limits: face run out, maximum: 0.1mm (0.0039in); radial run out, maximum: 0.13mm (0.005in)'. Furthermore, they say that the testing is performed with the chuck mounted on a standard insert. It is well to note, however, that wood is quite compressible – with different densities even in the same piece – and, depending upon its moisture content, may warp while turning; this is what makes working with wood so interesting. However, under these circumstances, expecting accuracies as quoted by the manufacturer is not realistic. For most woodturning situations, there is little need to achieve such tolerances, but it is nice to know that the chuck was built to provide them.

I've now purchased several Nova chucks and they have always performed very well, but I do not believe any chuck with the set of jaws supplied at the time of purchase will do everything that the average woodturner requires of it. I tried to get by with the 2in (50mm) jaws that came with my first Nova chuck, often attempting to hold a tenon that was too large for the jaws, but found that they damaged the tenon, because only the points of each jaw-segment were touching

Fig 9.2 **The basic Nova chuck and the two tommy bars that are used to open and close it**

the wood; they almost always held the wood, but such a grip does damage to all but the hardest of woods. I finally realized that to use the chuck to its fullest capability I needed a variety of jaws, and so have purchased several of the chuck jaws available for these chucks. It is nice to have a chuck set up with the particular jaws that you want when you need them, but it is not a difficult task to change the jaws on the Nova.

Many people complained about having to use two rods or a rod and a spanner to operate the Nova chuck; however, I find that, if you have a spindle lock, operation of the Nova chuck is a one-handed affair and is easier than using a key-type operation. The basic modification to improve the Nova chuck was to add gears to drive the scroll and allow a key to move the gears. This provided one-handed operation, a significantly greater grip, and resulted in another chuck from Teknatool called the SuperNova chuck.

The SuperNova Chuck

This has a body made from machine steel for strength and wear, and is protected by a nickel-plated finish. The SuperNova requires only one hand to operate and the geared action requires less effort for tightening. It is easy to support the work with one hand while tightening with the other. SuperNova's T-bar handle can swivel away, preventing collision with either the lathe or the turning. Fig 9.3 (below) shows a typical SuperNova chuck.

The gears on the SuperNova are hardened and the open back makes them easy to clean. I've had no problems with mine getting clogged and find that, generally, a shot of air will blow away any chips, and so on. The gear drive of this chuck provides more holding power for larger workpieces than the standard Nova chuck, making it possible to extend further from the face of the chuck, or to handle rough and uneven pieces.

*Fig 9.3 **The SuperNova chuck includes a T-bar handle to tighten and loosen the chuck, providing considerably greater closing force***

According to the manufacturer, the SuperNova, fitted with the PowerGrip jaws, can hold large bowls or platters up to the full 29in (740mm) diameter of the Nova 3000 in outboard operation. I have never tried to hold such large pieces with mine, but I have no doubt that it would handle the promised work-holding.

SuperNova is designed for use with a wide range of lathes. The manufacturer says that it is most suitable for lathes with a 16in (405mm) diameter swing. I have found that it works very well on lathes from small mini-lathes like the Carba-Tec and the Nova Mercury.

The SuperNova chuck is available with the standard 2in (50 mm) jaws that are normally supplied with the standard Nova chuck or with the PowerGrip jaws, which are not recommended for use on the standard Nova chuck. All of the jaws sets available for the Nova chuck will also work with the SuperNova chuck – one of the reasons that I purchased my first SuperNova chuck, as I already had two Nova chucks, a number of jaws for them, and a number of inserts to make the chuck fit onto different lathes; all of these accessories are interchangeable between the Nova and SuperNova.

The Nova Compac Chuck

High-quality chucks like the Nova and SuperNova are fairly expensive and can cost almost as much as a small lathe. The Compac chuck from Teknatool was designed and priced especially for users of the mini, midi and budget lathes, with up to 12in (300mm) diameter swing. Chucks designed for full-sized lathes don't fit so well on mini/midi lathes – their size and bulk just gets in the way, and they weigh more than one should normally put on small spindles.

The Compac weighs 10% less than the Nova, and 20% less than the SuperNova, making it ideal for smaller lathes. Although the Compac is a small chuck, it delivers comparable closing power to the Nova chuck. Most chucking projects appropriate to a 12in (300mm) diameter capacity lathe can be carried out with ease. You can purchase an adapter jaw accessory plate that will allow the range of smaller jaws for the Nova and SuperNova to be used; specifically, the Pin, 1in (25mm), 2in (50mm), Step, 1⅜ and 1¾in (35 and 45mm) spigot jaws.

I find the Compac chuck to be well engineered and pleasant to use. It is somewhat limited in range of jaw movement – ranging from 1⅜–1¾in (35–45mm) in compression mode and 1¾–2⅛in (45–53mm) in the expanding mode – but I find this range quite acceptable for the small lathe work for which it was designed (see Fig 9.4, below).

SuperNova Deluxe 5in (125mm) Chuck

This new Nova chuck from Teknatool puts their chucks into an entirely new league of turning (see Fig 9.5, below right). At 5in (125mm), a full inch (25mm) larger than its brother the SuperNova, this chuck is designed for large and heavy turnings. The workings are completely sealed, and the jaw mechanism is opened and closed with the large T-handled hex key included. The SuperNova Deluxe comes with the PowerGrip jaws, but accepts all the jaw sets from both the Super and Standard Nova chucks and a free chuck adapter insert is included. With the PowerGrip jaws the chuck can hold large work up to 29in (725mm) in diameter and also hold spigots up to 19in (475mm) long. It has a dovetail facility up to a 5in (125mm) recess. This is one heavy chuck and it works very well.

One complaint that many people had about the Nova chucks was the amount of the opening and closing range. Teknatool has solved the problem with the SuperNova

Fig 9.4 The Nova Compac chuck, especially designed for use on small lathes

Fig 9.5 The SuperNova Deluxe 5in (125mm) chuck is totally sealed; it is operated by a hex key, a new direction for this chuck line

Deluxe chuck. I purchased mine while in New Zealand and spent some time talking with the people at Teknatool. The chuck that I purchased has jaw-slides with only two holes to fit all of the existing Nova chuck jaws. The chuck will soon be equipped with new jaw-slides that have three screws to hold each jaw to the slide. This will provide even greater holding power. I was told that people who purchased the earlier release of the chuck will be able to upgrade easily and new jaw-slides will be provided for them with the new three-screw chuck jaws.

Jaw Accessories Available for the Nova Line of Chucks

The following list describes the various accessory jaws available for Nova and SuperNova chucks (see also Fig 9.6, below).

● **1in (25mm) Jaw Set**

This versatile jaw set is designed for a variety of small bowls (expanding dovetail) and projects with small spigots (contracting mode), generally below the size that can be handled by the standard 2in (50mm) jaws. The 1in (25mm) jaws can also act as a type of pin chuck, expanding the jaws into a 1in (25mm) bored hole for first bowl work.

● **1in (25mm) Nova Pin Jaw Set**

These special extended jaws are designed to act like a pin chuck, expanding into a pre-bored hole. This is an especially useful technique for free-form edge bowls. A great advantage over pin chucks, though, is that you don't have to bore to an exact size – any size between the minimum and just under the maximum expansion will do.

Fig 9.6 **Some of the jaws and accessories available for Nova chucks (from left): the 1in (25mm) jaw set; the woodworm screw; the PowerGrip jaws; the 5⅛in (130mm) jaw set, and the 2in (50mm) jaw set that is supplied with most of the Nova chucks.**

The longer jaws allow for a very powerful spigot grip for all smaller work up to 6in (150mm) in length, such as lace bobbins, delicate pots, and so on. The jaws also have a dovetail to mount small bowls up to 6in (150mm) diameter.

● Nova Spigot Jaws

These jaws are available in two different internal sizes, 1⅜in (35mm) and 1¾in (45mm).

They are designed to grip both in the contracting (gripping round or square spigots) and in the expanding mode with a workpiece up to 10in (250mm) long. They are ideal for long, unsupported hollow boxes and vases, and their serrated tooth form makes for a very powerful grip.

● Step Jaw Set

The step jaws are primarily to grip the base (foot) of footed bowls in the contracting mode. The step sizes provide optimum gripping for three foot sizes: 1²¹⁄₃₂in (42mm), 2in (50mm) and 2³⁄₆₄in (54mm). There is also an expanding-dovetail mode for alternative recess gripping of bowls.

● Cole Jaw Set for Remounting Bowls

This is a very versatile set designed primarily for the re-chucking of bowls to remove chuck marks, or for re-shaping the bottom of bowls that have already been turned. There is also provision to mount the 2in (50mm), step and 4in (100mm) jaws onto the Cole jaws, which enhances their use considerably. All the facilities of the other jaw sets can be fully utilized in conjunction with the Cole jaws. A special woodworm screw (optional) can be used for initial bowl mounting and,

with this combination of holding methods, it is possible to turn a bowl from a rough blank to a completely finished smooth bowl with just this one jaw set. There are a number of re-chucking options: false wooden jaws can be added, wooden dowels used, or rubber stoppers, which are provided with the basic kit.

> These Cole jaws, more than any others, really begin to explore the tremendous versatility of the Nova chuck.

● 4in (100mm) Jaw Set

This jaw set is designed for an expanded dovetail grip up to 14in (350mm) diameter, reverse dovetail grip for gripping footed bowls, limited spigot facility up to 6in (150mm) long, and provision to mount false wooden jaws, so customized jaws can be made for special purposes. They are made for a larger range of work than the standard 2in (50mm) jaws or step jaws.

● 5⅛in (130mm) Jaw Set

These jaws are designed to handle very large work up to 29in (735mm) in diameter. With these jaws you don't run out of capacity with the Nova chuck.

Other Accessories

● Spur Centre

This is a rugged, four-pronged spur drive with a ¾in (20mm) square shank, that fits snugly into the Nova chuck jaws. Creep of the spur is prevented, as the shank is slotted to allow the chuck jaws to close over it. The design takes quite a novel approach, with points located at each corner, and the wedged shape of the prongs allows them to penetrate and firmly grip the wood. The spur is the answer for turners who use the Nova chuck most of the time, but want to be able to swap quickly for spindle work.

● Woodworm Screw

The form of this screw has a deep, fine blade, which is machined right to the end of the screw, allowing an easy lead into the wood and the depth of the blades; the core size enables the mounting of the larger wood blanks onto the chuck. The screw – which is 1in (25mm) long, with blades $\frac{1}{16}$in (2mm) deep, and core size of $\frac{5}{16}$in (8mm) – has a square shank for positive locking into the chuck. The right-hand woodworm screw comes standard with the Nova chuck.

● Chuck Jaw-slides (set of four)

These come standard with the chuck. Many turners use extra jaw-slides to mount their accessory jaw sets; changing the accessory jaws is then as easy as unwinding one set of slides and winding in another set, with the accessory jaws already mounted.

● Cole Jaws Woodworm

Woodworm screw with the same specification as the screw listed above, but with an extra length for use with the Cole jaws.

● Chuck Spanner

This double-ended spanner is more than just a chuck accessory: as well as the large hex end, which can be used to remove chuck inserts, the smaller hex end is useful for the Comet, Nova 3000 and Ornamental Turner.

The Oneway Line of Chucks

Shortly after the Nova chuck appeared on the market, Oneway Manufacturing in Canada introduced the Oneway chuck, which looked very much like the Nova chuck and operated in the same manner. Since that time, Oneway have brought out two more, the Stronghold, and the Talon chuck, their most recent introduction. The Stronghold and Talon chucks are key-operated four-jaw self-centring scroll chucks, and the original Oneway chuck is a lever-operated four-jaw self-centring scroll chuck. Many accessories, such as optional jaw sets, woodworm screw, and drive centres are available for all of these chucks.

The Oneway Chuck

- This chuck is operated by two levers.
- There are four lever-holes in the body, and three holes in the scroll, a design which creates a constant differential and allows one-handed tightening.
- The levers are made from high-strength steel and will not deform or bend in use, thus preventing damage to the holes in the chuck.
- The chuck has a nickel-plated body and hardened base jaws with manganese phosphate-coated scroll, and a patented over-extension prevention system for added safety.
- The chuck has a zigzag base jaw-slide design which, according to the

Fig 9.7 **The basic Oneway chuck, which is very similar in operation to the Nova chuck**

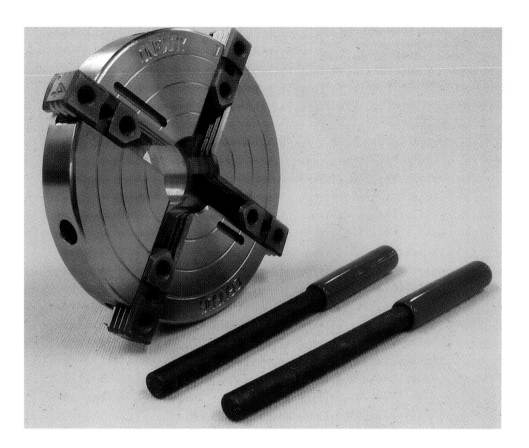

manufacturer, gives 50% more contact area and adds to the longer life and easier operation of the chuck.

- Oneway's No. 2 Jaws are included as standard, which provides external chucking (closing on a tenon) with a range of 1¾in (45mm) to 2in (50mm) and internal chucking (expanding into a recess) with a range of 3in (75mm) to 3½in (87mm).
- It has replaceable inserts to make it fit different lathe spindles.
- Sizes are available up to 1¼in x 8 tpi, but not for larger sizes.
- The chuck weighs approximately 4.5lbs (2kg).

The Oneway Stronghold Chuck

- The Oneway Stronghold chuck is operated by a key, providing two major advantages over the Oneway: one-handed operation and greater holding power.
- Like the Oneway chuck, the Stronghold has a nickel-plated body, hardened base jaws, and manganese phosphate-coated scroll.
- The Stronghold also has Oneway's patented over-extension prevention system for added safety, which prevents the jaws from being over-extended and therefore coming loose from the chuck during operation.
- The key is supported in two places for longer life and accuracy.

Oneway Chuck Accessory Jaws

Spigot Jaws (Talon and Oneway), No. 1 Jaws (Stronghold)

These jaws are called the No. 1 jaws for the Stronghold chuck, but can also be referred to as spigot jaws. They are machined long and deep for better grip on smaller parts, and the outside surface of the jaws is serrated to grip the workpiece.

No.1 Jaws

These are useful for turning small bowls, knobs, vases or spindles. Available for the Talon and Oneway chucks.

No. 2 Jaws

Available in two configurations: profiled jaws and smooth jaws. The profiled No. 2 jaws come standard on all Oneway chucks and the patented profile on these jaws provides extremely good gripping power on both square and round stock. The smooth jaws have the same capacities as the standard No. 2 jaws (and are offered at the same price) and the inside and outside surface of the jaws is smooth. They are designed, and recommended, for light cutting applications. These jaws will not mark workpieces as much as the standard No. 2 jaws, but will not grip with the same power, either.

No. 3 Jaws

These jaws have the mass and size necessary for producing large bowls and vases, and have Oneway's patented profiled jaw design. When turning large bowls, Oneway recommends using their 2in (50mm) Jumbo screw with these jaws, which are designed for use with the Oneway, Talon and Stronghold chucks.

No. 4 Jaws

These jaws have even more mass and size than the No. 3 jaws, described above, and are also designed for those turners producing large bowls and vases. When turning large bowls, Oneway recommends using their 2in (50mm) Jumbo screw with these jaws. The jaws are designed for use with the Oneway Stronghold chuck.

Jumbo Jaws

The Jumbo jaws are aluminum plates, 11in (280mm) in diameter, machined from solid stock for greater strength. Their unique combination of slots and tapped holes for mounting the rubber grippers enables the holding of an infinite number of round, oval or square shapes. Buttons are hard rubber, pressed over a tapered steel sleeve for superior holding; they are for use when making light finishing cuts on the backs of bowls and for external chucking on platters and picture frames. By using an extra button set, it is possible to stack buttons, which further accommodates odd shapes. Wooden false jaws may be mounted and turned for those requiring the utmost in precision finishing or for extremely large or critical applications.

Mini Jumbo Jaws

These are 8½in (213mm) in diameter, and for use on various smaller-sized lathes.

Mega Jumbo Jaws (Stronghold only)

Available in a larger 14in (350mm) diameter and can be used for much larger bowls.

Flat Jaws

Wooden blocks are screwed to the face
of these jaws, which can then be turned
to provide a custom-grip jaw set. Virtually
any turned shape can be gripped without
fear of marking.

Collet Jaws and Pads
(available for the Stronghold chuck only)

These jaws are designed to fit specific
diameters when making bottle stoppers, and
other components made from turned-to-size
round stock, such as dowels.

Vicmarc Family of Four-jaw Self-centring Chucks

The Vicmarc Uni-Chuck was the first four-
jaw self-centring chuck to be designed and
manufactured in Australia by Vicmarc
Machinery:

- It has the precision, simplicity and
  reliability of the engineering chuck
- Grips internally and externally
- Will hold round and square work
- Has a hollow centre, so through-boring
  can be done from either end
- Can be run clockwise or anti-clockwise
- Manufactured from K1045 (medium tensile
  steel), giving higher durability and
  ensuring a longer life and high-quality
  finish, which is less susceptible to rust.

Vicmarc chucks are available in four Models:
VM90, VM100, VM120 and VM140. The
VM90 and VM140 are lever-operated chucks
and the VM100 and VM120 are key-operated
chucks (see Fig 9.11, above right).

Fig 9.11 **The VM100 and VM120 chucks (right),
are operated with a T-bar Allen key. The two
on the left are the VM90 and VM140, both
operated by two levers.**

The VM90 and VM140 chucks are designed
for those who prefer to operate the chuck
using quick-acting tommy bars (levers).
I find these chucks are quick if your lathe
has an easily activated spindle lock, as then
the chuck provides one-hand operation.
If you do not, then it can be a bit tricky
holding two tommy bars and the work at
the same time.

The basic chuck, as purchased, comes
with chuck body, dovetail jaw set, two tommy
bars, screw point, Allen key, appropriate insert
to fit your lathe and owner's manual.

The VM90 has a diameter of 3¾in
(96mm) and weighs 3¾lbs (1.7kg), and
its compact size makes it ideal for use on
12in (300mm) capacity lathes or smaller.
With the standard jaws, it has a minimum
opening of 1⅝in (40mm) and a maximum
opening of 3¼in (80mm).

The VM140 will hold most work up to 20in (500mm) in diameter with standard jaws. It is a larger chuck, measuring 5½in (138mm) in diameter and weighing 9¼lbs (4.2kg). The jaw openings are also greater with a minimum opening of 2¼in (55mm) and a maximum opening of 5⅛in (130mm).

The VM100 and VM120 T-bar Allen key-operated chucks provide one-hand tightening, along with tremendous gripping power provided by the 6 to 1 ratio of the scroll. Keyed chucks cannot be beaten when it comes to holding power and the totally enclosed back assures consistent, smooth action by preventing dust and debris from getting into the scroll of the chuck. The backing lid is also indexed for those woodturners who do not have an indexing facility on their lathes.

The VM100's compact size makes it ideal for use on 12in (300mm) capacity lathes or smaller, whilst the VM120 will hold most work up to 20in (500mm) in diameter with standard jaws. The VM100 measures 3¾in (96mm) in diameter and weighs approximately 4lbs 10oz (2.1kg). With the standard jaws it has a minimum opening of 1⅝in (40mm) and opens to 3⅛in (80mm). The larger VM120 measures 5⅜in (136mm) in diameter and weighs 8½lbs (3.9kg). With the standard jaws it has a minimum opening of 2¼in (55mm) and a maximum opening of 4⅜in (110mm). The basic chuck includes chuck body, dovetail jaw set, T-bar Allen keys, screw point, knock out bar, appropriate insert to fit your lathe and owner's manual.

Accessory Jaws for Vicmarc Chucks:

A wide range of accessory jaws are available for the Vicmarc chucks. Some of these are shown in Fig 9.12 (facing page).

Step Jaws

These were designed by the famous Australian woodturner and author, Richard Raffan. They are effective for holding a range of spigot sizes with minimum jaw movement and without the need to change the jaws. Boxes are easily turned using the step jaws and the bottom of the box can be turned without leaving unsightly pressure marks, by holding its rim. The outside dimension of the VM90 and VM100 chuck jaws is 4in (100mm) while for the larger VM120 and VM140 the outside dimension is 5⅛in (130mm).

Pin Jaws – 1⅜in (35mm)

These pin jaws, designed by well-known American woodturner and author Dick Sing, are used for items such as kaleidoscopes and pepper grinders. They measure 1⅜in (35mm) outside with a minimum internal diameter of 5⁄16in (8mm). Available for the VM90 and VM100 only.

1in (25mm) Jaws

These jaws are used for expansion into small recesses and for firm holding of fine spindle work, such as earrings and chess pieces. They are ideal for turning salt and pepper shakers. They measure 1in (25mm) outside with a minimum internal diameter of 5⁄16in (8mm) and are available for all four chuck models.

Fig 9.12 **Some of the accessories available for the Vicmarc line of chucks (from left): screw faceplate; bowl jaws; and selection of faceplate rings.**

Long-nose Jaws

These jaws allow better access between the chuck body and the rear of the workpiece. They are also very practical when pre-turned or long workpieces have to be refastened. For example, when turning serviette rings or remounting rough-turned work. For the VM90 and VM100, the external diameter is 1⅜in (35mm) with a minimum inside diameter of ⁵⁄₁₆in (8mm). For the larger VM120 and VM140 chucks, the outside diameter measures 1⅞in (47mm) with a minimum internal diameter of ⁵⁄₁₆in (8mm).

Shark Jaws

Shark jaws are so-called because of their serrated inner and outer jaw surfaces and the extended jaws provide an aggressive hold. They hold cylinder spigots more safely than standard jaws and are available in 1⅜in and 1¾in (35mm and 45mm). For the VM90 and VM100 the 1⅜in (35mm) jaws have an

outside diameter of 1⅞in (47mm), while the 1¾in (45mm) jaws have an outside diameter of 2¼in (55mm). The VM120 and VM140 chucks have a larger outside diameter for these jaws. The 1⅜in (35mm) jaws measure 2⅛in (55mm) on the outside and the 1¾in (45mm) jaws measure 2¾in (68mm) on the outside. The standard internal spigot grip on each of these measures 1⅜in (35mm) and 1¾in (45mm) respectively.

Multi-purpose Jaws

By removing one or more of the dovetail segments from these jaws, they can be adapted to a variety of uses, and the wide range of expansion and contraction of the chuck provides for unique adaptability. External diameter for the smaller chucks is 5⅞in (148mm) and 8¼in (210mm) for the larger chucks.

Dovetail Jaws

These are designed for mounting bowls by expanding into a recess or clamping onto a spigot. The sizes indicated are the outside measurements of the jaw faces when fully closed. Dovetail jaws provide approximately 1in (25mm) of expansion beyond their specified size. For the smaller chucks this measurement is 4in (100mm) and for the larger chucks 5⅛in (130mm).

Dovetail Jaws – 2¾in (70mm)

These dovetail jaws were designed to accommodate work that varies between the standard dovetail jaws that are supplied with the chuck and the 4in (100mm) dovetail jaws. Outside diameter measures 2¾in (70mm) and inner diameter measures 2¼in (55mm). Available only for VM90 and VM100.

Bowl Jaws

These adjustable jaws allow the user to re-chuck bowls for finishing the bottom, or to do light clean-up work on the foot of the bowl. To mount, the bowl is reversed and held by the rim, either internally or externally, with eight unique, soft PVC stoppers which are mounted on the face of the jaws. These jaws are available in 11¼in (285mm) and 15⅛in (385mm) for the VM90 and VM100. On the larger chucks, VM120 and VM140, there are three sizes available: 11¼in (285mm), 14⁵⁄₁₆in (358mm) and 19¼in (485mm).

Additional Accessories for Vicmarc Chucks

Faceplate Rings

These can be used instead of the traditional faceplate. They facilitate remounting of prepared blanks by mounting directly onto the chuck jaws and can also be used for turning green wood, which will require re-turning later on. The rings fit standard jaws supplied on chuck. For the VM90 and VM100 they are available in 2¾in (70mm) and 4in (100mm) diameters. On the larger chucks, they are available in 5in (125mm) and 6in (150mm) diameters. Because of their design they only work well with Vicmarc chucks.

Screw Faceplate

The screw faceplate enables you to quickly remove the job from the chuck and remount if necessary. The dovetail on the screw chuck enables it to fit any Vicmarc chuck.

The Axminster Chucks

I have been able to find information on two chucks manufactured by Axminster Power Tool Centre: the Artisan chuck and the Precision four-jaw chuck. The Precision four-jaw chuck is basically an engineering chuck adapted to woodturning applications with threaded backplate to fit specific woodturning lathe spindles.

Artisan Chuck by Axminster

The Artisan chuck offers many of the
features found on the more expensive
Precision four-jaw chuck including single-
key tightening for one-hand operations. It is
compatible with all Axminster jaws and
accessories. The Artisan chuck is beautifully
finished, accurate and easy to use,
according to my source. The chuck uses
threaded adapters to fit to specific lathes,
and does not accept precision four-jaw
backing plates. The basic chuck includes:
chuck body, key-tightening handle, 2¾in
(70mm) dovetail jaw set and threaded
adapter insert (see Fig 9.13, right).

Axminster Precision Four-jaw Chuck

This chuck is a self-centring engineers'
chuck, originally designed to the tolerances,
precision and performance required by
machinists in the metalworking industry. It is
fitted with accessory-mounting jaws, which
accommodate all Axminster accessories.
The full range of jaws and accessories make
it one of the most versatile chucks on the
market today and it is the favourite of Ray
Key, one of England's finest woodturners.

I've seen Ray Key demonstrate a number
of times with the Axminster Precision four-jaw
chuck and he has purchased extra accessory
mounting jaws to which he has attached his
accessory jaws. He quickly screws out the
accessory mounting jaws and replaces them
with a new set containing the particular jaws
that he wishes to use. This is less expensive
than having eight or nine chucks each
fitted with different jaws, as I have in my
workshop. The basic Precision four-jaw chuck
includes: the chuck body, a threaded

Fig 9.13 **This Artisan chuck made by Axminster is a smaller precision chuck**

backplate to fit a particular lathe spindle,
a tightening key and a set of accessory
mounting jaw slides, but NB: you have
to buy a set of accessory jaws to make
the chuck usable (see Fig 9.14, below).

Fig 9.14 **The Axminster Precision four-jaw chuck is big and strong and has a wide range of accessories available**

Axminster Chuck Accessory Jaws

The Axminster family of chucks has about the widest range of chuck accessories of any of the makers of four-jaw scroll chucks (see Fig 9.15, below).

Accessory Mounting Jaws

Changing jaws can be quick and easy if you mount accessory-mounting jaws directly to the accessory jaws, and it eliminates the hassle of removing and replacing eight screws to change the accessory jaws. Simply back out the accessory mounting jaws and spin in the desired jaws that are mounted on their own set of chuck accessory jaws.

Fig 9.15 **Some of the Axminster chuck accessories (clockwise, from left): gripper jaws; accessory-mounting jaws; 1in (25mm) dovetail jaws; 2in (50mm) dovetail jaws.**

Dovetail Jaws

The dovetail jaws simply screw onto the accessory mounting jaws. 'A' dovetail is designed to expand into a 4in (100mm) recess and compress onto both 2⅜in (60mm) and 1in (25mm) spigots; 'B' dovetail gives expansion into a 2½in (62mm) recess and compression on a 1in (25mm) spigot; the 'C' dovetail jaws expand into a 2¾in (70mm) recess and have a specially lipped internal grip on a 2¼in (55mm) spigot making them ideal for endgrain work, such as boxes and goblets; 'D' dovetail jaws are for small work-holding. They are dovetailed for gripping internally and have a plain bore for spigot holding. The two sizes of dovetail offered are 1in (25mm) and 1½in (38mm) respectively at their optimum internal dovetail grip and ½in (12mm) and ¾in (20mm) for their central bore.

Type G Gripper Jaws

These are 4½in (112mm) outside diameter, 3½in (87mm) inside diameter. The jaws are ¹¹⁄₁₆in (17mm) deep with serrated inner jaws for extra grip.

Type 'H' Gripper Jaws

Similar to the type 'G' jaws, these provide unequalled work-holding, especially for large diameter pieces. The main gripping surfaces are serrated on the internal and external walls and also on the central spigot grip.

Type 'BF' Gripper Jaws

Similar to the type 'H' gripper jaw, but the 'BF' offers the same power for smaller diameters. Optimum sizes are 1⁷⁄₁₆in (36mm) externally and ¾in (20mm) internally, the internal serrated grip extends for 1³⁄₁₆in (30mm), giving excellent gripping power on spigots.

O'Donnell Jaws

These jaws give access around the jaws for close-in tool work and have a deep recess for holding long spigots and giving solid mounting when turning a long way from the headstock without tailstock support. The jaws are also dovetailed both inside and outside on the lip. Three sizes are produced: 1in (25mm), 1½in (38mm) and 2in (50mm). The size stated is the nominal bore of the spigot recess.

Cylinder Jaw

When turning long and thin projects it is a great advantage to be able to grip a blank along a substantial amount of its length, to impart a good measure of stability to the workpiece. The Axminster cylinder jaw chuck was designed to do this. It has a parallel-sided jaw with either 1in (25mm) or 2in (50mm) cylindrical bore. In addition to the spigot-holding of this jaw, Axminster has added an external and internal dovetail to each giving 2⅜in (60mm) and 2¹⁄₁₆in (52mm) on the larger 2in (50mm) chuck, and 2⅜in (60mm) and 1⅛in (27mm) on the smaller 1in (25mm) jaw.

Havita 'Plus' Jaws

The Havita 'Plus' dovetail jaw expands into a 2⅜in (60mm) recess. The inside lip of the jaw has a special ⅜in (10mm) radius to grip a 1⅛in (28mm) decorative spigot.

Havita Soft Edge Jaws

The Havita Soft Edge jaw has a standard dovetail on the expansion side of the jaw, its optimum size being 2⅞in (72mm) and a radiused grip on the inside. This enables the turner to produce a finished decorative spigot with a ¼in (6mm) cove and hold this accurately and firmly without damage to the finished piece.

Internal Accessory Jaws

This jaw set is a stepped version of the Axminster accessory jaws. It extends the variety of the standard bolt on jaws available. It is available as an internal or an external stepped jaw.

Internal and External Jaws

Additional stepped jaws to increase the versatility of the Axminster range of woodturning chucks.

Spigot Jaws

These are second-generation spigot jaws, modified to create an enhanced grip, which have been designed to cope better with the vagaries of a firm grip in green wood. Similar to a pin chuck, you bore a 1in (25mm) hole 2in (50mm) deep into the log or blank, and insert the chuck jaws to the full depth – it is essential that the whole length of the jaw is inserted, to avoid over-stressing and damage to the jaws – then open the jaws to effect a firm grip on the blank. Should this loosen as you work, another tweak on the key will re-establish the grip. If you wish to hold even larger pieces of wood, Axminster offers a Super Spigot jaw requiring a 2in (50mm) hole to a depth of 1⅝in (40mm).

4in (100mm) Wood Jaw Plates

These are a set of pre-drilled steel quadrants onto which self-made wooden jaws can be mounted. They can be used for re-chucking

to remove a dovetailed recess or spigot, or producing movable jam-chuck-type holding devices.

6in (150mm) Wood Jaw Plates

When made up as bowl-gripping jaws, these give extra hold to large lumps of wood. The increased diameter obviously gives more support to the rear of any self-made large diameter wood jaw. However, for anything up to 12–14in (300–350mm) diameter, the standard 4in (100mm) diameter plates described above should be more than adequate.

Button Jaws

These jaws use eight conical buttons – which are made from white rubber to avoid marking the workpiece – to securely pull back work onto the jaws. The buttons are 'dovetailed' to hold the workpiece firmly against the plates.

Machined to mount directly onto the standard accessory jaws, the 6in (150mm) button jaws are intended for use with bowls up to 9in (225mm) in diameter. Larger sizes are available in diameters of 10in (250mm) and 16in (400mm).

Button Jaws are, however, unsuitable for bowls with a very fine edge, because the point pressure will deform the edge of the bowl.

To hold large or thin-edge bowls, use the wood jaw plates as described above, affixing four quadrants of timber to the jaws and turning a recess to exactly match the outer diameter of the bowl to be finished. However, using the button jaws on thicker bowls, or more substantial work, provides a quick and accurate way to hold and finish endless projects without marking or damaging the work in any way.

Mega Jaws

These new jaws are the largest dovetail jaws available for the Axminster system. They stand at a huge 5in (125mm) on the external diameter, and will hold more than a 4in (100mm) dovetail internally to a depth of ⅝in (16mm), so are ideal for large platters, and so on.

Other Axminster Chuck Accessories

Faceplate Ring

These rings are made to match the dovetail jaws, and negate the need for a separate faceplate to mount a bowl blank on, prior to turning the outside. Simply screw the ring to the chosen blank and expand the dovetail jaws into it. Available for 'A', 'B', and 'C' dovetail jaws.

Eccentric Chuck

The eccentric chuck is designed to fit onto the 'C' dovetail jaws, in a similar way to the faceplate ring. The moving plate is made from aluminium to reduce the weight and consequently the eccentric forces. The plate may be moved clockwise or anti-clockwise, using four positions in each direction, in order to give an unusual approach to turning. To add further scope to your original designs created by using the eccentric chuck, try using the Tony Witham eccentric spiralling attachment (see top right).

Eccentric Spiralling Chuck

This chuck is an adaptation of Tony Witham's original idea. Tony has enhanced the Axminster production to provide a spiralling capability in addition to the original eccentric capabilities.

Screw Chuck

This is a replaceable stainless steel parallel screw, mounted onto a boss which fits into either the 2½in (62mm) recess of the 'A' dovetails or the 1in (25mm) recess of the 'B' dovetails. It is also available to fit the internal recess of the 'C' dovetail jaw.

Pin Chuck

These are turned from solid bar on the cam principle, which allows a larger-than-normal locking bar to be used, giving very positive holding power in even the softest of woods. They are available in four sizes: ⅝in (16mm), ¾in (20mm), 1in (25mm) and 1½in(38mm) and can be gripped either in the stepped jaws, or on the 'nosed' portion of the accessory mounting jaw. The two larger sizes have a conical drive bored in their centres.

Record Power RP4000 Geared Scroll Chuck

The growing desire to provide a single-key four-jaw geared scroll chuck has prompted Record Power to bring out their RP4000 geared scroll chuck. It is available to fit ¾in x 16 tpi or 1in x 8 tpi lathe spindle sizes. The chuck comes with the chuck body, a carrying case, two 'T'-handles, indexing plate, woodscrew, and the standard jaw set expanding from 1¾–3⅜in (45–84mm) and

Fig 9.16 The Record Power RP4000 geared scroll chuck

contracting from 1¾in (45mm). Like the other four-jaw scroll chucks on the market, there are a number of accessory jaw sets to fit this chuck (see Fig 9.16, left).

Accessory Jaws

A number of accessory jaws are available for the Record Power RP4000 chuck. Some of these are shown in Fig 9.17, below.

Dovetail Jaw Set

Provides expansion into a recess from 4⅞–5½in (123–138mm) and contraction onto a spigot from 3⅞–3½in (97–88mm).

Multi-purpose Jaw Set

By removing one or more of the dovetail segments from these jaws provides expansion into a recess from 4¼–5⅛in (108–130mm) and contraction onto a spigot from 3⁷⁄₁₆–2¾in (86–69mm). In their literature

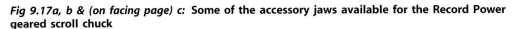

Fig 9.17a, b & (on facing page) c: Some of the accessory jaws available for the Record Power geared scroll chuck

Record also indicate that it provides expansion into a recess from 6⅝–7⁷⁄₁₆in (166–186mm) and contraction onto a spigot from 5¾–5in (145–125mm), but it is not clear whether these are step jaws or two different sizes.

Shark Jaw Set

Provides expansion into a recess from 2⅞–3⁷⁄₁₆in (72–86mm) and contraction onto a spigot from 1¾–1⁵⁄₁₆in (45–33mm). A larger size of this jaw set is available that provides expansion into a recess from 3⅛–3⅝in (80–92mm) and contraction onto a spigot from 2–1⁹⁄₁₆in (50–39mm).

Long-nose Jaw Set

Provides expansion into a recess from 1⅞–3¼in (47–80mm) and contraction onto a spigot from 1⁵⁄₁₆–⁵⁄₁₆in (33–7mm).

Step Jaw Set

Provides expansion into a recess from 3⁵⁄₁₆–5½in (84–138mm) and contraction onto a spigot from 3¾–1⅝in (96–40mm).

Pin Jaw Set

Provides expansion into a recess from 1¹³⁄₁₆–2½in (47–63mm) and contraction onto a spigot from ⅞–¼in (22–6mm).

Adjustable Bowl Jaw

This set of jaws is available in two sizes: the smaller set has a maximum diameter of 11⅜in (288mm) and the larger set has a maximum diameter of 15⅜in (390mm).

The Longworth Chuck

Leslie Douglas Longworth (a member of the Hunter Valley Turners' Club, based in Newcastle in New South Wales, Australia) developed the Longworth chuck, which was designed to hold a bowl in order to decorate or remove the chucking marks on the bottoms of bowls and platters. His design was documented in two articles that were published in his club newsletter before he died in 1988.

Because the design of the chuck was given to the woodturning community as a whole, appearing in various publications, it could not be patented, which made it less interesting for companies to bring it to production. Until now, if you wanted a Longworth chuck you had to make it yourself or talk someone else into making one for you, as they simply were not commercially available; but finally, Lloyd Johnson of Woodturner PRO, LLC, has

decided to market them (see Fig 9.18 on page 86). Lloyd was experimenting with making a centring jig for gluing segmented rings to a previous glued-up portion of a vessel, and found that a modified form of the Longworth chuck worked very well. Here are the specifications of the Longworth chuck from Woodturner PRO, LLC:

- The chuck is made from two polycarbonate discs (rather than the wood, as was used for the original Longworth chuck), one $\frac{1}{2}$in (13mm) and one $\frac{1}{4}$in (6mm). Polycarbonate is the material from which bulletproof glass is made, so it is strong and nearly indestructible. Less expensive materials are available of course but, in the interest of safety, this material was a great choice.

- Arcs are routed into the discs to accept $\frac{1}{4}$ x 1$\frac{3}{4}$in (6 x 45mm) hex-head bolts. The $\frac{1}{2}$in (13mm) disc is routed on one side to allow the hex head to be recessed into the disk and slide, but not twist in the channel. This recessed channel allows the disk to be mounted flush to the table of the centring jig.

- Four rubber bumpers hold the item to be turned. As wing nuts are tightened, the bumpers expand, yielding holding power that is sufficient for holding the items for which the chuck has been designed.

- The $\frac{1}{2}$in (13mm) disk has been drilled and tapped to fit faceplates that have countersunk 2$\frac{3}{8}$in (60mm) or 2$\frac{7}{8}$in (72mm) on-centre holes (a faceplate is included in the Longworth chuck

configuration). The disc is mounted to the faceplate using 10–24 $\frac{7}{8}$in (22mm) long, flat-head machine screws.

- There is a 1$\frac{5}{16}$in (33mm) hole drilled in the centre of both discs. These holes have been sized to allow a 1in (25mm) PVC Schedule 40 pipe to fit loosely within the hole. This allows the discs to be placed on the surface of the centring jig around a PVC plunger.

- To maintain proper registration when used as a lathe-mounted Longworth chuck, a threaded centre stud, 1$\frac{5}{16}$in (33mm) in diameter, is used.

- The chuck is available in either a 9$\frac{1}{2}$in (237mm) or 13$\frac{1}{2}$in (337mm) diameter.

Assembling the Longworth Chuck

1 First, put the faceplate on the lathe, to check that it will work on the lathe spindle and that the threaded centring stud will fit into the faceplate.

2 Mount the faceplate to the four threaded holes on the $\frac{1}{2}$in (13mm) polycarbonate disk – the routed curves have a recess on one side of the disk. Put the recessed part face-down on the workbench, screw the threaded stud into the faceplate, and then slip this stud extending from the face of the faceplate into the hole in the centre of the $\frac{1}{2}$in (13mm) disk. Rotate the faceplate until four holes align with four threaded screw holes in the polycarbonate disk. Insert screws and tighten.

3 Screw the faceplate onto the lathe spindle and apply the ¼in (6mm) polycarbonate disk so that the threaded locater stud slips through the centre hole of the disk, then insert the ¼in (6mm) machine screws through the rubber bumpers.

4 Assemble in the following way: bolt, washer, large end of the rubber bumper, another washer, insert bolt through intersections of the curves in the two disks, another washer and then a wing nut. The rubber bumper should be on the side facing the tailstock.

5 The chuck is opened and closed by rotating the two disks, which causes the bolts with the rubber bumpers to move out or in, depending on the direction of rotation. I recommend using some protection between the tailstock and the bowl, so that the bowl is pressed gently against the face of the chuck while rotating the two disks to bring the rubber bumpers against the surface of the bowl. Then tighten the wing nuts down to secure the bowl in place. As the wing nuts are tightened, they compress the rubber bumper and cause them to expand against the bowl. All wing nuts should be tightened – as near as possible – by the same amount.

Safety Points

Here are some safety points to keep in mind whether you have purchased the chuck from Woodturner PRO LLC or made your own:

● With the chuck mounted on the lathe, set the spindle speed to 600 rpm or less.

● There is a pinch-point between the bed of the lathe and the chuck when the 9½in (237mm) model is used on a 10in (250mm) swing lathe and when the 13½in (337mm) model is used on a 14in (350mm) swing lathe.

● The wing nuts should never be oriented to the exposed side of the chuck, as there is a great chance of injury to fingers. Clothes can snag on the wing nuts and the bolts, so great care should be taken to keep clothing away from the chuck.

● Never use the chuck to grasp an item if its wall profile is expanding where the rubber bumpers meet the item, unless the tailstock fitted with a revolving centre is in contact with the item in such a way that it is impossible for the work to come free from the chuck.

● The only safe way to use the chuck is with the centre stud in position.

Fig 9.18 **The Longworth chuck. This is now commercially available, but can still be made by craftsmen who like to make their own tools and accessories**

Because of the large plate-type jaws, such as the Nova Jumbo jaws, produced by most of the makers of four-jaw scroll chucks, and the development of the vacuum chuck, which is discussed in Chapter 10, the need for this type of chuck has decreased. I am including it here because there are many woodturners who don't use four-jaw chucks and would like to have something to hold their bowl to finish the bottom. There are also many who like to make their own tools. The following part is for those woodturners.

Making the Longworth Chuck

Basically, the Longworth chuck consists of two disks mounted together on a rotating pin or bolt, so that they can rotate separately. One of the disks is mounted onto a faceplate to fit the lathe on which it is to be used. Curved slots have been cut into the two disks so that three or more bolts riding in the slots can move from the most inner diameter of the slots to the

most outer position of the slots as the disks are rotated. These bolts incorporate a rubber stopper that moves with them along the curve. There can be as few as three slots and as many as the disks can safely accommodate. I believe that most people use four slots. Fig 9.19 (facing page) is an edge-view drawing showing the composition of the Longworth chuck.

This just about describes the chuck in terms of its components. The most critical part of the construction is accurate layout and cutting of the curved slots. The two plates consist of a piece of fibreboard and a piece of plywood. The one 'A' hole is drilled through the centre of this construction for mounting the piece of ¼in (6mm) birch plywood, to create a sandwich of the two disks. A ⅜in (10mm) bolt should be used to mount the plywood to the fibreboard backboard. Then nail the plywood to the backboard at several places that would be close to the rim of the chuck.

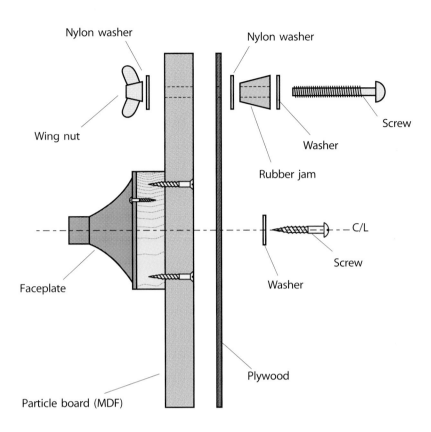

Fig 9.19 **The composition of the Longworth chuck**

Mount the fixture onto the lathe spindle; turn it round, then lay out three circles and draw them onto the face of the disk. The first or smallest circle is the diameter of the faceplate waste block, which should be turned to the diameter of the faceplate. Draw a circle about ¾in (20mm) in from the outside edge of the plates. The third circle is centred between the two circles.

Place the toolrest at lathe-centre height and engage the indexing pin. Draw a horizontal line across the centre of the disk. Rotate the lathe spindle 90˚ and draw a second line perpendicular to the first, which passes through the centre of the circle. If you

don't have an indexing plate on your lathe, you can do this off the lathe. Draw a line passing through the centre of the plate.

Then, using a set square or a pair of dividers, mark out another line perpendicular to the first one. Where these two lines intersect in the middle of the circle, make an indent. These four indents are the centre points for a circular segment to be cut by the router.

Use a compass to draw circular segments that begin at the horizontal centre line on which one of the indents was made. The radius of this circular segment is the distance from the indent point to the opposite side of

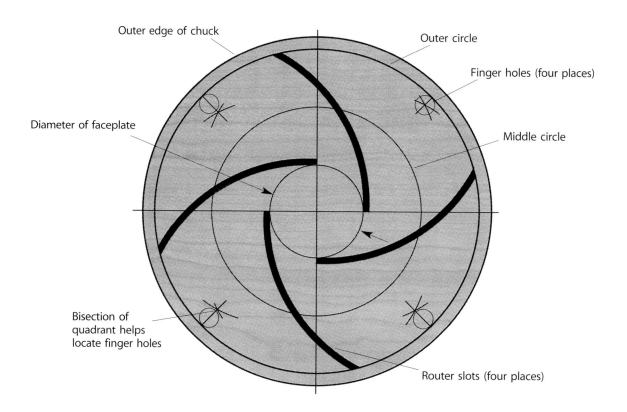

Outer edge of chuck

Outer circle

Finger holes (four places)

Diameter of faceplate

Middle circle

Bisection of
quadrant helps
locate finger holes

Router slots (four places)

Fig 9.20 **Laying out the scroll for the Longworth chuck**

the smallest-diameter circle. This arc is swung
from the centre line up to the largest circle, as
shown in Figure 9.20 (above). This line marks
the inside edge of the router cut. Do this four
times from each of the indents that you made.

Now, set the compass to scribe another
line so that there are two lines that are as far
apart as the width of the bolts to be used
in the slots. The space between these two
lines is the area to be routed or cut out. If
a router isn't available, they could be cut
with a scroll saw and the slots cleaned up
with a file. I recommend using a router bit
the same diameter as the bolts to be used.
Drill a small hole through the two boards at

each swivel point (the indents that were
made earlier) and locate a swivel point on
the router table that would make the router
cut between the lines drawn to indicate the
router path. I recommend drilling a hole at
each end of the area to be cut: the first hole
at the centre line marks the start of the cut;
the hole at the large circle marks the end
point. Repeat this with light cuts for each
slot until all slots are cut through both
boards. Finally, drill four finger holes in
between the slots and bordering on the
outer ring. The finger holes are actually on
lines that bisect the four quadrants (see
Fig 9.20, above, for this layout).

Remove the nails that hold the plywood disk to the backing board, flip it over and re-attach it with a centre screw. All that remains is installation of the four bolts with washers and rubber jaws and a wing nut on the back side, as shown in Fig 9.19 (on page 87).

To use this new chuck, mount it on the lathe, loosen the wing nuts and rotate the two boards in opposite directions to open the space between the rubber jaws, allowing your bowl to be placed between them, face down on the plywood disk. Now, rotate the two disks to close up the rubber jaws onto the rim of the bowl. Snug it up and tighten all four wing nuts. Your bowl and chuck should look like Fig 9.21, below.

There you have it – a four-jaw scroll chuck that you can make yourself. You should keep the speed of the lathe down while using this chuck and only make light cuts. It was designed to use in cleaning up the foot or bottom of bowls and not for doing heavy-duty turning.

Author's note: the information contained in this chapter was obtained from the sales literature or the websites of the various manufacturers. The information about the making of the Longworth Chuck was obtained from the author's More Woodturning website: http://www.fholder.com/Woodturning/chuck.htm

Fig 9.21 **The commercial Longworth chuck mounted on the lathe with a bowl clamped in its jaws ready to turn the foot of the bowl**

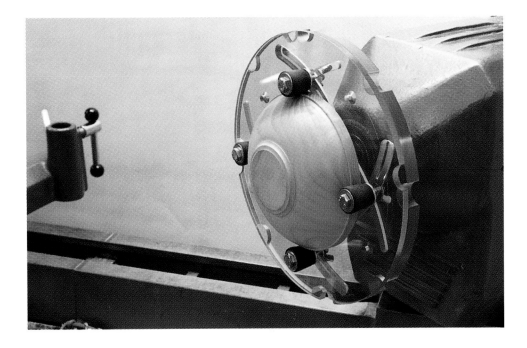

10 The Vacuum Chuck

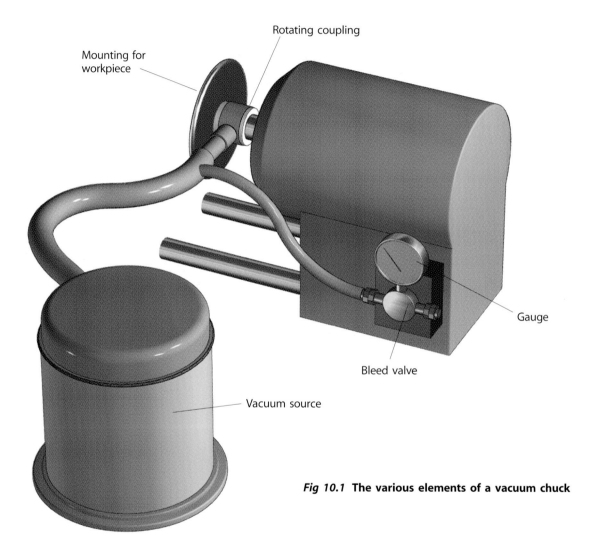

Mounting for workpiece

Rotating coupling

Gauge

Bleed valve

Vacuum source

Fig 10.1 The various elements of a vacuum chuck

The vacuum chuck is one of the most recently developed methods for mounting wood on the lathe and it is gaining more devotees. It is designed for reverse chucking bowls and hollow forms, to clean up and final-turn the foot. It will hold a wide range of shapes and sizes of project and various means of obtaining a vacuum seal can be used.

It is a fairly simple method of holding work and is very effective. As shown in Fig 10.1, the vacuum chuck consists of a vacuum source, a hose to connect the vacuum source to the lathe, a rotating connector to connect the hose to the rotating spindle, and a plate or cup to form the join between the item being held and the lathe spindle. This latter is actually the chuck, which provides its holding power by evacuation of the air between the object and the lathe spindle: the object is held onto the chuck by ambient air pressure, somewhat less than 15lbs psi. The larger the size of the object and the area of the joining chuck, the greater the pressure against the chuck face, and hence the greater the holding power of the chuck. This holding power is increased as the vacuum between the two surfaces is increased and, as the diameter of the object is decreased, a greater level of vacuum is required to hold it, because of the decreased surface area.

My first encounter with the vacuum chuck was at a demonstration by Soren Berger of New Zealand at the Utah Woodturning Symposium in Provo, Utah, in 1997. Apparently, Soren had been making his vacuum chucks and selling them for some time and I believe that his system was the only one commercially available on the market at that time.

He was using the simplest of vacuum sources – the workshop vacuum extractor/cleaner normally used to clean up the workshop – and the rotating connector was made from PVC pipe and a couple of sealed bearings. Soren had fitted a piece of wood with a hole drilled through it to the lathe outboard end of the spindle, and taped it to his PVC rotating connector with duct tape. His chucks came in several sizes and consisted of a piece of wood mounted to a faceplate, with a cardboard cylinder attached to the piece of wood. A rubber seal on the edge of the cylinder provided the seal for the workpiece to be mounted; you could easily hold a natural-edge bowl with his vacuum chuck, because the cylinder was long enough to move the bowl rim away from the headstock. Since that first encounter, I've heard of many ways to make home-made vacuum chuck systems.

Old automobile air conditioner compressors were a very common vacuum source in the early days of the vacuum chuck development. Vacuum pumps have been around for years in industrial applications, so it wasn't too long before used vacuum pumps came onto the market and, shortly thereafter, new purpose-built vacuum pumps began to appear. Also, rotating connectors became available to connect the vacuum source to your chuck. Most of these look similar.

The most common adapter that I've seen is the E-Z vacuum chuck adapter sold at several woodturning suppliers in the United States. This consists of a threaded rod that slips through the through-bored headstock spindle, a self-centring, rotating air fitting that connects to the rod on the handwheel side, and a No. 2 Morse taper vacuum fitting that fastens to the rod on the other end (see Fig 10.2 below).

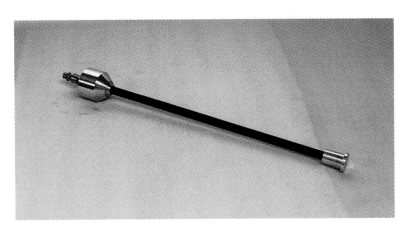

Fig 10.2 **The E-Z vacuum chuck adapter is the most common rotating connector on the market**

The rod is actually a piece of hollow, threaded lamp rod, which is used in lamps to pass the wire to the lighting fixtures, which are threaded for this size of rod.

The E-Z vacuum chuck adapter comes with instructions on making a properly designed vacuum chuck using a standard faceplate, a section of 2in (50mm), 4in (100mm), or 6in (150mm) diameter PVC pipe and a foam seal. This system will require a vacuum pump for proper operation – the instructions say that a workshop vacuum will not work. That is true with the smaller diameters; however, my wife had purchased one of the E-Z vacuum chuck adapters and I made up a connector that would connect our small one gallon (4.5ltr) workshop vacuum to the connecter on the E-Z vacuum chuck adapter outboard end.

We made a flat faceplate disk with a piece of mouse pad material glued to the surface, and this held bowls that were 6in (150mm) or larger with no problem. We ultimately purchased a more powerful Gast vacuum pump and as it provided more suction, it did work considerably better.

Actually, my first venture into vacuum chucking was using a vacuum plate designed by Vic Wood of Australia, and manufactured by Vicmarc (see Fig 10.3, below). This system was designed for use on lathes without a through-bored spindle, and I first saw it demonstrated by Vic Wood at Puget Sound Woodworking Center in Everett, Washington, in 2001. The vacuum plate was designed to work with a vacuum cleaner and fitted my one gallon (4.5ltr) workshop vacuum nicely. It is designed with the foam pad extending beyond the edge

Fig 10.3 The Vicmarc vacuum plate, designed by Vic Wood of Australia, uses a vacuum cleaner as the vacuum source

of the 11in (280mm) aluminum plate, so that larger bowls can be effectively held with the plate extending into the inside of the bowl; I found that it worked very well on pieces 6in (150mm) and larger. The workshop vacuum was very noisy, however, and made me seek a less noisy vacuum source.

We saw Soren Berger of New Zealand demonstrating again, this time vacuum chucking small objects at the Utah Woodturning Symposium in 2002, and he was using one of the Gast vacuum pumps to provide the vacuum for his system. It was a very quiet pump, and this motivated me to buy one. He was using one of the E-Z vacuum chuck adapters, except that the Morse taper piece had been replaced by one turned out of white plastic material.

Soren had turned an extension on the Morse taper fitting to accept a short length of garden hose, which extended through the four-jaw chuck into the base of a small wooden cup that was held in the chuck. The edge of the cup was coated with hot-melt glue, allowed to set, then turned and sanded smooth. The hot-melt glue seemed to make an excellent seal between the chuck and the workpiece and he was holding very small items, less than 2in (5mm) in diameter, very firmly.

The Oneway Manufacturing Vacuum Chuck System

Oneway Manufacturing consulted Dave Lancaster on the design of their new drum chuck, after seeing him use a vacuum chuck in his shop in Maine. Oneway does not sell a system, but sells all of the components that

Fig 10.4 **The Oneway Manufacturing vacuum cup chuck – the author's favourite**

are needed to assemble a vacuum chucking system – i.e. drum chuck, rotary air adapter, gauge kit and vacuum pump – and woodturners can buy any one of these to use when assembling their own system (see details below). The Oneway aluminum drum chuck is illustrated in Figure 10.4, above. This has the best interface with the wood to be held that I've seen.

To use the Oneway products to build a vacuum chuck system, the lathe must:
1. Have a through-hole in the headstock spindle.
2. Be threaded at the outboard end.
3. Have no cross holes drilled through the spindle.

The Oneway Components for their Vacuum Chucking System:

Oneway Drum Chucks

These are made from aluminum, and the rim is covered with neoprene so, unlike the drum chucks made of cardboard tubing or wood, they are non-porous, will always run true, are long lasting, and have adapters to fit most lathes.

A taper lock adapter (the same adapter as used for the Oneway Stronghold chucks) is supplied with Oneway drum chucks. The great advantage of using an adapter is that the drum chuck can be made to fit almost any spindle size, and will fit other lathes by simply changing the adapter.

The Oneway drum chucks come in three sizes: 3½in (87mm), 5½in (138mm) and 8in (200mm) and Oneway recommend using the largest chuck that a piece will fit. The 5½in (138mm) one is the most suitable for new users of the vacuum chuck, as it is the most versatile for bowls in diameters of 6in (150mm) or more. Anything less than 6in (150mm) in diameter can safely be turned on the small – 3½in (87mm) – drum chuck, which is their latest addition; it is designed to fit any size of lathe, and comes with a former, adapter and neoprene seal. Oneway recommends it for turning small spheres, such as croquet balls. The 8in (200mm) drum chuck cannot be used on pieces less than 8in (200mm) in diameter.

Rotary Adapter

The rotary adapter allows a vacuum to be drawn through it, while preventing the hose from spinning with the spindle – the key to a good vacuum system. However, as highlighted above, to use the Oneway rotary adapter, the lathe must have a through hole in the headstock spindle, it must be threaded on the outboard end, and it must have no cross holes drilled through the spindle. A taper lock adapter, as described above, is supplied with Oneway rotary adapters.

Gauge Kit

The gauge kit includes everything you need – mostly off-the-shelf items that Oneway purchases and assembles for resale as a kit – plus a bracket for convenient mounting of the gauge. A bleed valve is included, to reduce the vacuum in the system; this is necessary because, if one had a perfect seal in the system, the vacuum pump would continue to increase the vacuum until the full capacity of the pump was being applied and, in many cases, this would be sufficient to crush the vessel being held by the vacuum chuck.

A vacuum pump that will draw a minimum of 20in (510mm) of mercury is required, and the one that Oneway sells is ¼ horsepower and will draw 26½in (670mm) of mercury.

Craft Supplies USA Artisan Vacuum Chuck System

Craft Supplies USA doesn't manufacture anything, but they have assembled all of the components for a vacuum chuck system (see Fig 10.5, facing page). Their kit – for that is what it is – includes a backing board to be screwed to a faceplate, three sizes of PVC pipe fitted with a foam seal on the top, an

E-Z Vacuum chuck adapter, and a Gast vacuum pump. They do have a vacuum gauge kit, which will allow you to monitor and control the amount of vacuum being used, but this is an optional accessory and does not come as a part of the the kit. This is the system that I finally purchased, and it does give a more secure holding of smaller works than that obtained from the Vicmarc vacuum plate that I purchased first. This kit has simply done the shopping for you and glued on the foam seal, but there is still some work to get it operational.

Both the Oneway system and the Craft Supplies system require a bored-through headstock spindle and are unusable with lathes having a solid headstock spindle, such as the Record Power lathes and the Poolewood lathes. These lathes could, however, use the vacuum plate designed by Vic Wood, because it does not require a drilled-through headstock spindle as it applies the vacuum at the operator end of the spindle.

The Vicmarc vacuum plate was never commercially available in the United States and I had to purchase mine from an Australian firm, Southern Woodturning Supply, which is now called Carba-Tec ACT. A check of their website shows that they are still selling the Vicmarc vacuum plate. Another system, manufactured in the United States, has recently become available that works in the same manner, but does not limit you to a flat plate; this system, called VacuuMaster vacuum chuck assembly, is manufactured by the Sierra Mold Corporation, in Carson City, Nevada, USA.

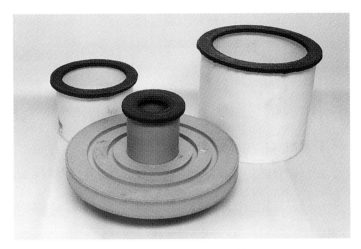

Fig 10.5 **The Craft Supplies USA vacuum kit**

The VacuuMaster Vacuum Chuck Assembly

The VacuuMaster vacuum chuck will fit on any lathe, or will transfer from lathe to lathe, by means of an adapter similar to those used by scroll chucks on the market today. This chuck has been designed so that all the works are forward of the headstock, in a self-contained unit (see Fig 10.6, below).

Fig 10.6 **The VacuuMaster vacuum chuck was designed for lathes with no hole through the headstock**

The VacuuMaster vacuum chuck assembly comes with connecting hose, threaded adapter, and the necessary hardware and Allen wrenches to assemble the chuck. Optional items are faceplates and vacuum bells and they list threaded adapters for 1in x 8 tpi, 1¼in x 8 tpi, and 33 x 3.5mm threads. At the time of writing, I've not seen these available in any catalogue or woodturning supply store, but they are listed at the company's web address and can be purchased direct from them.

Using the Vacuum Chuck

One of the most common uses of the vacuum chuck is for remounting of the bowl or platter for final turning of the foot, to clean up all of the marks left by the scroll chuck or faceplate used to hold the bowl while turning. Aligning the vessel properly on the vacuum chuck is a bit of a problem, unless you have some method of centring. Vic Wood, of Australia, demonstrated the use of a Morse taper mounted spindle thread that works wonders. You simply remove the workpiece, chuck (or faceplate) and screw the chuck onto the threaded part of this Morse taper mounting arrangement.

Oneway Manufacturing has made an adapter that screws onto their live centre for the tailstock and accomplishes the same thing. Figure 10.7 shows a photo of this adapter with the spindle thread on its end.

Fig 10.7 **A Morse taper adapter made from the Oneway live centre and their special threaded adapter screwed onto the threads of the live centre**

Fig 10.8 **The Morse taper adapter holding a bowl ready to apply to the vacuum chuck**

Figure 10.8 shows how the bowl is mounted onto the tailstock ready to be applied to the vacuum chuck.

I generally start smaller bowls between centres so that the foot of the bowl has a centre point that aligns with the centre of the foot of the bowl. When remounting the bowl for final turning of the foot, I simply use the tailstock live centre to help position the bowl onto the vacuum chuck. This works very well as long as you ensure that the tailstock is centring the work just before it is applied to the vacuum chuck.

In the case of production work of similar pieces, it is possible to make up special mountings to align the work on the vacuum chuck. In a Nick Cook demonstration of platter turning at the St Paul, Minnesota American Association of Woodturners Symposium in 2001, Nick stated that he had recently completed a large run of similar platters for a customer (I believe he said 2500 of them), and that he band-sawed each platter blank to precisely the same diameter. He then had a vacuum chuck mounting to align the blank to the vacuum chuck while he turned one side. He would turn a large number of one side of the platters, then he used another vacuum chuck mounting that accepted the platter – turned to a precise diameter – for turning of the other side of the platter. He had used the vacuum chuck for all turning on this large order of platters and said that he could not have produced them as quickly as he did without the vacuum chuck.

A great many of the people using vacuum chucks do not bother with a gauge to measure the amount of vacuum they are pulling. This is not too much of a problem unless you are turning very thin bowls and vessels, but I have talked with a number of turners who stated that a thin wall without reduced vacuum will often collapse.

One further warning, especially in winter turning, is the possibility of a power cut and a flying bowl when the vacuum ceases to exist. I recall one turner running his vacuum through a pressure tank, so that a volume of vacuum remained to allow time to catch the vessel before it went flying across the room. Personally, I use the tailstock as much as possible, both to help support the vacuum chuck, and as a back-up in case of a power cut. I slip a small piece of endgrain wood between the bottom of the bowl and the tailstock live centre to prevent or reduce the damage to the foot of the bowl. In cases where I already have a detent from the live centre during initial turning, I simply use this, gradually reducing it until there is a very small point of a cone holding the tailstock in contact with the bowl. This will usually be sufficient to prevent a flying bowl in the event of a loss of power.

One final comment on the use of a vacuum chuck: it cannot be used on vessels with holes whether they are worm holes, natural voids/fissures, pierced, or woods with a very porous grain. I have even heard of people losing vacuum due to leakage through the bottom of endgrain-turned vessels.

11 Eccentric Turning Methods

The earliest forms of eccentric turning were done between centres, and were known as multi-centre turning – a form of mounting wood to provide sculptural shapes that has probably been used for many years. Briefly, I will describe this method of mounting and remounting on different centres to create some very nice work.

Using multi-centre turning, it is possible to turn many-sided pieces, such as boxes with three, four, or more sides, an oval piece such as required for a hammer handle, or simply crankshaft-type pieces to decorate the stems of goblets, and so on. The key here is to use a live tail centre with a cup centre for holding the wood. The drive should be with a dead centre cup centre or a Stebcenter, as these cup centres provide a better grip and help prevent splitting of the wood.

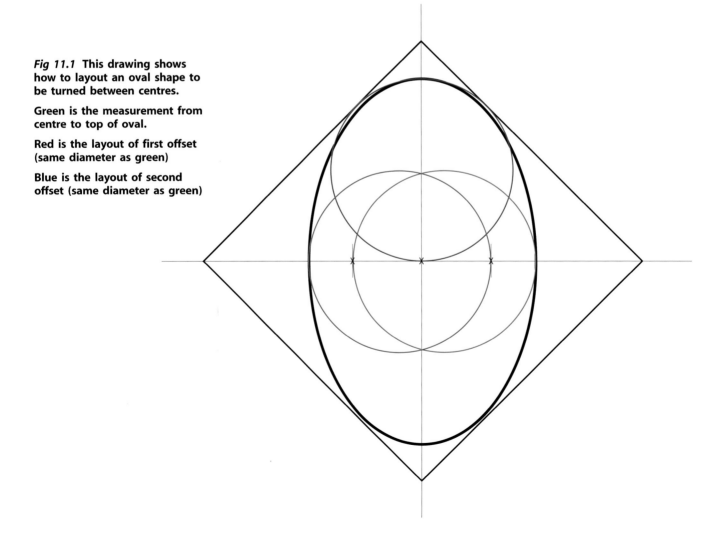

Fig 11.1 **This drawing shows how to layout an oval shape to be turned between centres.**

Green is the measurement from centre to top of oval.

Red is the layout of first offset (same diameter as green)

Blue is the layout of second offset (same diameter as green)

Multi-centre Turning

First, layout the location of the centre points and draw an oval of the shape and size desired in the following way, referring to Fig 11.1(on the facing page):

1 If the wood is square, draw diagonal lines between opposite points, to provide the axis lines for the oval.

2 Next, measure from the centre point to the highest point of the oval. Set a pencil compass to this dimension, then place the point of the compass on the narrow side of the oval on the centre line, and make a mark on that centre line.

3 Move to the opposite side of the oval and repeat this operation. These two points are your offsets for turning the piece oval.

4 Repeat this layout exactly on the opposite end of the wood.

5 Now mount the wood on the centre marked by the 'X' and turn it round, bringing the diameter to the diameter of the oval at its largest dimension.

6 Draw a line along the workpiece at the top of the largest dimension of the oval. Do this on both sides of the workpiece.

7 Offset the centre points to one side. Move the same direction on both headstock and tailstock centres, then turn until you are almost to the lines you

drew. Shift the workpiece to the other offset point and repeat this operation.

8 The workpiece is now nearly oval. Return the piece to centre position, sand with a strip of coarse sandpaper to round over the points, and the workpiece is oval.

9 If the workpiece is to be tapered, this must be done before turning the offset, and the oval on the small end must be of an appropriate size to fit in the head of the hammer. The end result should be a tapered oval like a hammer handle.

When using this form of work-holding, it is important to design the shape that you want and mark out the end pattern to accommodate the design. A similar form of multi-centre turning can be done using a faceplate with a number of locations laid out. This becomes more complex and requires a larger piece of wood on each end of the workpiece.

It is possible to do multi-centre work when holding the wood with a chuck that has serrated jaws, such as the Oneway Stronghold. In this case, the wood is turned round to fit the chuck jaws, then gripped firmly so that the serrations dig into the wood, and the piece extending from the chuck is then trued to its mounting. The chuck may then be loosened and the wood cocked so that the jaw serrations fit into different serrations on the wood. Tighten the wood and it rotates in an eccentric manner. This is not as precise as some of the following chucks discussed.

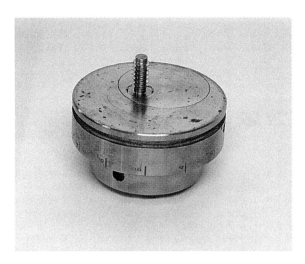

Fig 11.2 **The Robert Sorby eccentric chuck**

The Robert Sorby Eccentric Chuck

This chuck is big, sturdy and heavy and it needs a big lathe to handle it properly (see Fig 11.2, above). I've used it on a Carba-Tek lathe for demonstrations, but it is much too heavy for that small lathe.

Robert Sorby says it is a sophisticated chuck for multi-centre turning. To get more basic, it consists of a steel disk over 4in (100mm) in diameter and about 1½in (38mm) thick; the back side is recessed and threaded to accept the RS60BK back body, which is used to mount the chuck to your lathe; the back body – which is supplied as a part of the chuck price, but must be specified for a particular lathe – is also drilled and threaded to fit your specific headstock spindle; for example I ordered the back body to fit a ¾in x 16 tpi to fit my Record Power CL-3 lathe.

The front side of the RS60 disk has a 2⅜in (60mm) off-centre hole bored in it that is recessed about 1in (25mm); a snug-fitting insert, the eccentric or offset boss, fits into this hole. The back part of this insert is tapered slightly from the back, down to a point more than halfway to the front. This tapered surface is the area where two set screws mounted in the chuck body meet the insert to hold it in place and, once the set-screws are screwed in, the insert cannot come out.

The face of the insert has an offset hole – called the bi-hexagonal socket – that is machined to have 12 points part way through, with a recessed screw coming in from the back side to hold one of three supplied inserts. One of these inserts is a ⁷⁄₁₆in (11mm) diameter wood screw that makes the RS60 into a screw chuck, the second is half of the hexagonal ball drive mechanism, and the third is an adapter to hold a Premier chuck body. Each of these inserts has six points so that they are held firmly in position once inserted in the hole. They are kept from working out by the recessed machine screw in the back side of the eccentric boss. They can be positioned, with respect to the chuck body in 12 different positions (i.e. rotated in 30° increments). This gives you a sort of indexing system within the position of the chuck body.

There is a groove machined around the chuck body, slightly back from the face. This groove is not just for decoration: it intercepts the outermost part of the offset boss hole, creating a window in the chuck body that looks upon a part of the offset boss. An index mark on the chuck body can now be aligned with marks on the offset boss to provide some measure of positioning.

I say some measure, because you can never intentionally return the chuck to the same position, however hard you try – the adjustment simply isn't that precise.

The marks on the offset boss are in '0', '5', '10', and so on, up to '35'. These numbers indicate the amount of offset in millimetres, i.e. a setting of 5 indicates an offset of 5mm and so on up to 35mm. For people who don't convert or think in 'mm' that's a maximum offset of about 1³⁄₈in.

As you will gather, this is a complex piece of equipment and it is a sophisticated chuck for multi-centre turning.

Although I tried the first two drive mechanisms (I don't have a Premier chuck, so I can't try the Premier chuck adapter), the method that most appealed to me was the screw chuck. The hexagonal ball and socket drive is for spindle work and, although I do a certain amount of spindle work, I prefer faceplate-mounted work, with the tailstock used only for additional support on long pieces. Therefore, almost all of my work with the RS60 has been using the screw-chuck type of mounting. For this work, Sorby recommends that the timber used be a maximum ratio of 3 to 1, which means that a 4in (100mm) diameter piece could be 12in (300mm) long before you need to use the tailstock for support. But let me tell you, a 4in (100mm) diameter by 12in (300mm) long piece of wood offset 1³⁄₈in (35mm) and running at 500rpm is a spooky thing. What's more, if you've screwed into endgrain, it really is dangerous.

I've avoided the problem of endgrain mounting by gluing the endgrain turning blank to a cross-grain waste block; this makes a pretty secure mounting. Most of the time, I've been turning medium-size pieces

Warning

Safety is always important, but it is even more important with offset turning; you will be turning in the shadow area and catches are easy to make if you do not pay full attention to what you are doing.

The safety tips Sorby give in the instruction book supplied with their eccentric chuck caution the reader on safety. Their tips do not just apply to this chuck, but are standard for all turning as far as I'm concerned:

1. **Rotate the workpiece by hand before switching on the lathe.**

2. **Use the lowest lathe speed available initially. You can speed up later after you are sure the wood you are using and the mounting will handle a higher speed.**

3. **Always wear suitable eye protection, either safety glasses or a face mask.**

and my waste blocks have been made from sections of fir or pine 2 x 4in (50 x 100mm), but on a few of the larger pieces that I turned, I used a waste block of maple for added strength. The hole for this screw chuck should be $\frac{5}{16}$in diameter by 1in deep (8mm diameter by 25mm deep). I rough down the timber at a setting of '0' offset. It's hard enough to work on offset pieces that are already round without having to also work on knocking off corners.

The RS60 can be used to create polygonal sections with either the screw chuck or the bi-hexagonal socket. One can make up to a dodecahedron (12 equal sides), but each side will have at least a slight curve. This is where the 12 points in the offset boss come in; it is necessary to remove the offset boss to access the back and remove the screw, so that the screw chuck insert can be rotated a number of degrees and then reinstalled. It's a complex procedure, but then most complex turnings require complex procedures to accomplish them.

I have used the hexagonal ball drive and socket only once. That was to turn a hammer-handle-type piece that was completely round at one end (the tailstock end) and completely oval at the other end (the chuck end). I didn't care too much for

A couple of pointers that Sorby give apply to any screw chuck mounting and any work that will change its centre of rotation to finish it up:

- Always work towards the headstock. If you are turning a goblet or any offset piece, you need the strength of the unturned timber to progress down the stem. Let the turned portion 'swing in the breeze' so to speak.

- Always sand and polish each section of the workpiece before moving it to its new centre (as I said earlier, you can't return to exactly the same offset position once you've left it, so finish the turned part before moving the chuck to another setting).

I would like to add a couple more points:

- When turning something like a goblet – or anything where the turning is changing from a much larger section to an offset section – make sure that there is a small extension that is on the same centre with the larger part; if you fail to do this, there will be problems with the transition from the large part to the offset part.

- Use a gouge, but use it almost like a scraper – i.e. with the shaft of the gouge nearly horizontal – as it is very easy for the gouge to grab when working in any other position. People who think the skew is scary should try to use it on offset work!

this between centres eccentric turning, so I didn't do any more; however, I know that the capability exists if I need it to make some specific project.

Not having a Premier chuck, I could not check out the RS60 with a Premier chuck mounted on it in an offset configuration. This thought is even more scary. You not only have wood rotating off-centre, but you now have a metal chuck also rotating off-centre, a real knuckle banger! However, I'm sure it is perfectly safe, or Sorby wouldn't have made such an arrangement available.

The Escoulen Ball and Socket Chuck

I had followed Jean François Escoulen's exploits in the various woodworking and woodturning publications for some time and saw him demonstrating his ball and socket chuck at the AAW Symposium in San Antonio, Texas (1997). A year or so later I saw that the Escoulen chuck was available in the United States and I bought one (see Fig 11.3, below).

The first thing that I made with this chuck was a finial that could be used on the top of a box – or possibly an urn – using the following method:

1 Mount the piece of wood between centres on the lathe, and turn it round.

2 Then, using a parting tool and a ¾in (20mm) sizing gauge, turn a tenon on one end that is about ⅝in (15mm) long and slightly tapered towards the end. (The instructions say to press the wood into place with the tailstock, but I found a plastic mallet with the chuck setting on the bench was very effective.)

3 Next, mount the chuck onto the lathe, loosen the screw used to secure the ball in the socket, and use the tailstock to place the wood on-centre.

4 Tighten the set-screw so that the wood rotates on centre, turn the wood perfectly round for its entire length, and then turn a top finial on it; this could be any shape that pleases you – I chose to make it a teardrop shape.

5 Loosen the locking screw, and rotate the ball off-centre about one graduation, retighten the set-screw and turn the area to the left of the V-cut previously made at the bottom of the top finial. (This wood cut clean enough, so I did not need to sand.)

Fig 11.3 **The Escoulen ball and socket chuck**

N.B. You must sand at each stage before the chuck is adjusted, and after the turning is completed, as you will never be able to set the chuck back to where you want to sand later. One turner I know likes to sand the sharp edges of the turning with the lathe stopped, because you are less likely to take off the nice sharp edge with the piece still.

With each setting of the chuck, make the next cut on the left side of the part just cut (you can no longer cut on the part that was cut with the previous setting of the chuck). You can continue this down with different offsets, or you can loosen the 'P' pivot screw, rotate the ball in the socket one or more of the six indentations, and then reset the angle and secure the locking screw.

The Kel McNaughton Eccentric Faceplate

The Kel McNaughton eccentric faceplate, (see Fig 11.4, below), is solidly constructed of three different plates or segments. The first plate is a strong steel faceplate for work attachment, and has been designed with numerous screw holes to ensure adequate attachment and safety. The second plate (which accepts the first plate) is held captive between two rails of a third plate, which is covered with a guard disc, and the plate can slide between the rails, thereby allowing varying degrees of offset. It can also be rotated and held in various positions. The third plate (in which the second plate is captured) screws into the lathe spindle. At the back of this plate are two large weights, which can be shifted to various positions to provide counterbalancing for off-centre or out-of-balance work.

The weights are mild steel with a total weight of 12lbs (6kg), and the overall diameter of the eccentric faceplate is 10in (250mm),

Fig 11.4 **The Kel McNaughton eccentric faceplate (centre) is shown with the faceplate removed (lower right-hand corner), the Kelton balancer (left) and the angled faceplate (upper right-hand corner). Used together, they provide a complete eccentric faceplate, offering both sideways shifting and tilting of the workpiece.**

which nicely suits lathes with a 6in (150mm) swing or larger. The primary use for the eccentric faceplate is in turning off-centre work. Vases with off-centre necks are an exciting option, as are turnings with off-centred hollowing, creating variable wall thickness. Aside from this, the faceplate is excellent for turning out-of-balance work at speeds, which allow the wood to be cut properly.

Ian Durrant Offset Chuck Adapter

I first encountered Ian Durrant's offset chuck at the Craft Supplies Show in September 2001 (see Fig 11.5, below). This chuck adapter enables one to move the chuck, or faceplate, holding the workpiece to a different position, providing the offset capability that is sometimes needed to create a particular piece. If you don't wish to use a chuck or faceplate, you can use the multi-positioned drive centre for between-centres offset turning. The chuck allows you to select an offset with nine different positions around the centre, and also provides a considerable offset at two of these locations towards the rim of the adaptor. With all of the other multi-centre chucks that I've used, the wood is mounted directly to the chuck or to a glue block mounted onto the chuck; this device is a bit different, in that your chuck or faceplate is mounted to the offset position that meets your needs of the moment.

This chuck adapter, which screws onto the lathe spindle, is made from a one-piece aluminum casting, but is machined on all surfaces. The rear of the unit has a threaded boss, which contains the internal threads to fit

a specific lathe spindle. As the chuck is rotated, one will note 12 grooves around the outer ring of the body, which are used for indexing.

On the face of the chuck adapter, there are nine threaded holes to accept either the threaded stud for mounting a chuck or faceplate, or the four-prong drive centre. None of these holes is located on-centre. You can return to the same offset setting by replacing the stud into the same hole, but you can never turn exact centre with the lathe spindle. Why would you want to? This is an offset adapter, designed to offset the work. These holes are threaded for ¾in x 16 tpi inserts. There is also a series of concentric grooves cut into the face, and these grooves help you decide which hole the stud should be screwed into to give the desired amount of offset.

There are two holes in the rim of the adapter to accept a bar, and this can be used to loosen or tighten the chuck adapter to the lathe spindle. Both the threaded stud and the four-prong drive are drilled to accept

Fig 11.5 **Ian Durrant's offset chuck adapter**

a smaller bar, for loosening and tightening them into the face of the adapter.

The threaded stud will have a ¾in x 16 tpi thread on one end and then a different-size thread (one to fit the lathe spindle and therefore the lathe's chucks and faceplates). The instructions state that the ¾in x 16 tpi is the most popular spindle size for lathes. That was true a few years ago with the Sears lathe being one of the strong hobby lathes and the large number of Record lathes in use, which still use the ¾in x 16 tpi thread size.

In addition to the threaded stud, a four-prong drive centre is provided which will screw into the nine holes for using the device for offset turning between centres. Actually, most multi-centre work is done with the wood mounted in the spindle mode, i.e. with the grain of the wood running parallel to the axis of rotation. This sort of drive allows for considerable offset at the headstock end of the spindle, up to about 1¾in (45mm) of offset. With a minimum of offset being about ³⁄₁₆in (5mm).

Axminster Eccentric Chuck

The Axminster eccentric chuck is designed to fit onto the 'C' dovetail jaws of an Axminster four-jaw chuck, in a similar way to their faceplate ring. It may work best with the Axminster chuck, but I've found that it works fine with my SuperNova chuck with the 2in (50mm) jaws. The chuck consists of a back plate, which is gripped by the chuck jaws, and a moving plate to which the workpiece is attached. The moving plate is made from aluminum, to reduce the weight and, consequently, the eccentric forces. The plate may be moved clockwise or anti-clockwise, by four positions each way from centre, in order to give an eccentric approach to turning (see Fig 11.6, below).

For its simplicity, this chuck offers some unusual capabilities. It is also well machined and allows the return to a previous position easily and positively.

The instructions list the normal safety warnings: rotate the workpiece to make sure it doesn't hit anything before switching on the lathe, and use suitable eye and face

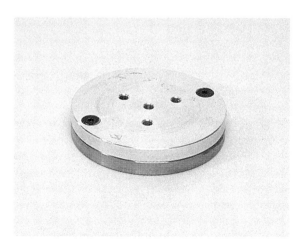

Fig 11.6a & b **The front and back of the Axminster eccentric chuck**

protection. They also recommend using the lowest speed in the beginning, until you have a better understanding of how to work with offset turnings, and verifying that your timber will withstand these stresses. The manufacturer recommends the use of a waste block against the face of the chuck onto which the workpiece is glued, or gluing directly to the chuck with hot-melt glue; but if you follows these instructions, you will have hot-melt glue on the face of the faceplate, and will lose the ability to rotate the workpiece 120° three times. When it comes to inlaying pieces into the end of a piece of wood or top of a box, this 120° shift-capability is needed to give a cloverleaf effect.

Eccentric Chuck Adapter from Craft Supplies

The Craft Supplies eccentric chuck is designed to be gripped by any four-jaw chuck that can expand into a 3in (75mm) recess (see Fig 11.7 below), and has two options for holding work. The standard equipment is a screw chuck that can be moved up to 1in (25mm) off-centre, but it is also available with a small faceplate, which can be attached to a waste block – the workpiece is then glued to the waste block using a suitable glue. Each revolution of the adjusting screw moves the centre of rotation one millimetre off-centre.

Fig 11.7 **Eccentric chuck adapter from Craft Supplies**

12 Other Forms of Chucking

In addition to the many methods of holding work on the lathe described in the previous chapters, there are other special forms, of mounting that do not fit into any of those specific categories, which I have gathered together in this chapter.

The Mini Gripper

This is a handy little chuck that quickly fixes small items to the lathe spindle without the use of tommy bars, spanners, chuck keys and so forth (see Fig 12.1, below). It is very quick and easy to use, and is especially suitable for people doing production work of small items such as boxes, goblets and so forth.

It requires a small recess in the base of a bowl, box, or other workpiece, which can be drilled with a Forstner type of bit using a drill press. This hole must be precise, because the mini gripper has a very small range of expansion. Once the hole is drilled in your workpiece, you simply slip it over the mini gripper until it bottoms in the hole, and twist. The chuck will hand-tighten to give you good holding power.

> The mini gripper is most effective in harder woods, as the fibres of wet woods or softer woods can be easily compressed, so the chuck might not be able to hold the piece securely.

Fig 12.1 The mini gripper chuck comes in two versions – one screws onto the ¾in x 16 tpi spindle threads and the other is mounted on a Morse taper adapter (either No. 1 or No. 2) to enable it to fit different spindle sizes with that Morse taper.

The mini gripper that I purchased several years ago to use on my Record Power mini-lathe was fitted with a ¾in x 16 tpi thread, so that it could be screwed onto the spindle nose. When I sold the Record lathe, I purchased another one that was fitted with a No. 2 Morse taper. It came with a collet to fit a 1¼in (32mm) hole, but additional collets can be purchased to fit 1in (25mm) and 1½in (38mm) holes. I find this chuck very useful when working with small objects that have enough waste wood available to accommodate the hole required for the chuck collet.

The Oval Turning Chuck

I'm not sure whether there are any oval turning chucks available in the marketplace at present, but I have been advised that Vicmarc is working to bring one to the market, developed by Johannes Volmer in Germany, probably by the time this book is published (Fig 12.2, below, shows the basic components of an oval chuck).

Many people have made their own oval turning chucks over the years, but instructions for the making of one is far beyond the scope of this book. I mention it only for people who wonder how those oval picture frames were made in the past. There is a very good discussion on oval turning in John Jacob Holtzapffel's book, *The Principles & Practice of Ornamental or Complex Turning*, published in 1884. This book has been republished in the USA by Dover Publications, Inc., New York.

The Centre Steady

The centre steady is a work-holding device that may be used on the outboard end of a hollow form, when the length is such that support at the base will not provide the proper amount of stability. Centre steadies can be purchased from some lathe manufacturers, as well as from a number of

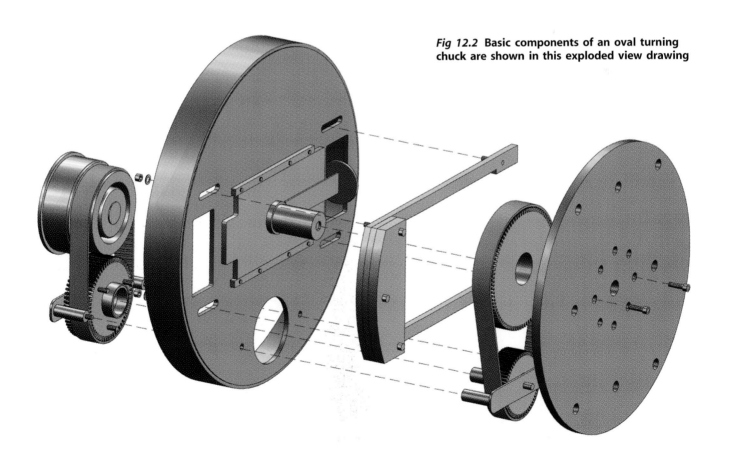

Fig 12.2 Basic components of an oval turning chuck are shown in this exploded view drawing

Fig 12.3 **The centre steady with three wheels running on the rotating wood**

companies who make them to fit on almost any lathe. My centre steady was made by John Nichols of Stanfield, Oregon (see Fig 12.3, left). John makes them in a number of sizes up to 22in (550mm) inside diameter and tailors them to your particular lathe. He uses three arms, 120° apart, with inline skate wheels mounted on each arm to ride against the wood. These are also excellent, when turning long spindles, for reducing the likelihood of vibration, or bowing of the spindle. Many people make their own from plywood or hardwoods, using the inline skate wheels to roll against the wood.

When turning extremely thin spindles, a string steady is quite useful. I have seen both Jean François Escoulen and Dave Regester using these when turning long thin spindles. Fig 12.4 (below) shows one of these string centres. You cannot purchase them, but they are fairly easy to make if you have a need for one.

Fig 12.4 **A string steady used in turning very thin and very long spindles**

The Doughnut Chuck

The doughnut chuck is a home-made device, used when turning the foot of bowls. It consists of a wooden disc – generally of plywood – mounted to a faceplate, and a second disc of plywood with a hole in the centre. The two pieces are held in position with three or more bolts with wing nuts. The plywood backing-disc can be covered with some form of foam padding, both to protect the bowl and to keep it from slipping. It is also good if foam is mounted around the hole in the top or doughnut disc to prevent marring the underside of the bowl.

In use, a bowl is carefully centred on the backing plate, and the top disk with the hole is mounted over it and properly secured with the bolts and wing nuts. The bowl is then firmly held in place, while the foot is turned and finished. Fig 12.5 (right) shows a simple doughnut chuck in use. I've seen Vernon Liebrant of Everson, Washington, who turns very large bowls, use the doughnut chuck to finish off the foot on his bowls. He turns a groove in the backing plate that just fits the bowl rim, and then secures the bowl in place with a doughnut disc and two bolts with wing nuts. Vernon's backing plate is generally a flat board, about 8 or 10in (approx. 200 or 250mm) in width. His doughnut disk is a sheet of unbreakable plastic he purchased as an offcut.

The Child Coil Chuck

The coil grip chuck was first made in 1972, but it was superseded a few years later by expanding chucks for bowls. Now that

Fig 12.5 **The doughnut chuck is used to hold bowls firmly while the bottom is turned. These are easy to make, but the one shown here is commercially available from Woodturner PRO, LLC.**

'hollow vessels' are in vogue, the coil chuck comes into its own: it could have been purpose-designed for deep-hollowing projects; it is quite capable of holding the largest projects that most lathes will handle, but it is also very handy for small projects such as goblets and vase forms. A typical project for this 4½in (115mm) diameter chuck would be the 14in high, 10in diameter (approx. 355 and 250mm) vase shown at the website of Peter Child Woodturning (http://www.peterchild.co.uk).

To prepare the wood to fit the chuck, simply make a spigot 3½in (90mm) in diameter and put a groove in it; the chuck contains a coil spring, which is forced into the groove when the chuck is tightened, and the spring pulls the wood firmly back into a 3½in (90mm) recess in the chuck, to lock it rigidly in place. (This chuck is available from Peter Child Woodturning Supplies – see the Appendix.)

The Fred Holder Ball and Egg Chuck

For the last few years, the Chinese ball has captivated me and taken up a lot of my workshop time. The ball chuck that I originally made had four screws to pull down the cap and hold the ball in place and, in the process of making a Chinese ball, one had to loosen and tighten the cap a number of times; this was time-consuming, so I made up a new ball chuck with a screw-on lid made out of elm. It worked pretty well, but I had problems getting the lid to tighten properly onto the ball; a thin washer cut out of a plastic coffee-can lid solved the problem and this chuck sped up the operation of making the Chinese ball.

The threads needed to be stronger, however, so I looked for an alternative way to make a screw-top chuck and I found a PVC plumbing compression coupling that appeared to provide exactly what I needed (see Figure 12.6, below).

In my new design, I used a 2in (50mm) compression coupling for the shell of the chuck, a piece of elm for the inside, and a Oneway Stronghold chuck insert to make it fit my lathe spindle. I turned a recess in the block of elm to accept the tapered Stronghold chuck insert. I then held the insert in place with two short drywall screws.

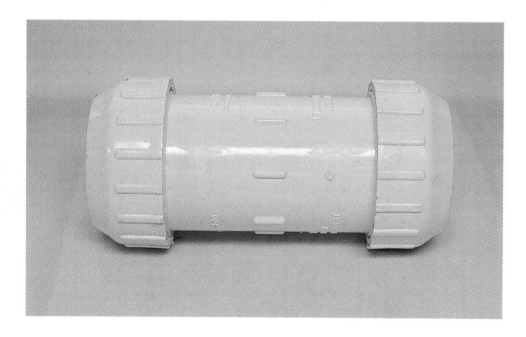

Fig12.6 **The PVC plumbing compression coupling is the basis for the ball chuck**

I screwed the insert onto the lathe spindle and turned the wood to fit into the coupling from the insert end, so that there was not a gap between the wood and plastic at the threaded end where there was a flare-out to match the rubber compression washer. When I had a very snug fit, I glued the wood into the plastic fitting with medium-thick Hot Stuff CA glue. Since this type of glue tends to be brittle and the joint could be broken with a sharp jolt, like a catch, I also added two drywall screws just ahead of the chuck insert, but far enough to the rear so as not to be into the hemispherical shaped recess in the end that accepts the ball.

I then turned a hemispherical recess in the end of the elm, turned a ¼in (6mm) thick piece of birch plywood to fit loosely into the screw-on lid, and screwed the whole thing together.

Next, I turned a hole in the plywood disk, with a chamfer on the reverse side to fit the shape of the 2½in (62mm) ball. The hole was opened enough to allow enough ball to extend through for the Crown tool handle to ride against while cutting. Figure 12.7 (above) shows the completed chuck.

It worked very well and the next nine Chinese balls that I made came out with a full five levels, as many as the Crown tools will allow one to make. This chuck was well-received at my demonstrations at the Crafts Supply Show in Bakewell in September 2001, and at my later demonstrations in Wales and New Zealand.

I have subsequently made a chuck along the same lines – but designed to hold eggs instead of a 2½in (62mm) ball – and it works very well for finishing the ends of wooden eggs (see Fig 12.8, right).

Fig 12.7 **The completed ball chuck and its components**

Fig12.8 **The egg chuck made along the lines of the ball chuck.**

The Die Chuck

Basically, this chuck is very much like a screw die. It is designed to screw onto the lathe spindle, and then to screw onto a tenon on the wood that it is holding. The die chuck is a simple method for holding material being worked on a woodturning lathe. The chuck is shown in Fig 12.9 (below).

> With the die chuck, wood must be mounted in the spindle-turning mode, i.e. with the grain running parallel to the axis of rotation.

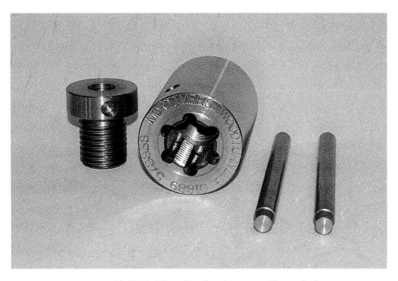

Fig12.9 **The die chuck uses a threaded recess to hold the wood onto the chuck. A Morse taper adapter is also available so that the user can turn between centres without removing the chuck from the lathe.**

To begin turning with the die chuck:

Mount the wood between centres, turn a 1⅛in (28mm) diameter spigot to the wood, 1³⁄₁₆–1⅜in (30–35mm) in length, and then turn a square shoulder at the point where the spigot joins the turning blank.

I recommend:

a) Turning a slight taper at the very end of the spigot, so that it will be easy to start screwing the spigot into the die chuck.

b) Wiping a thin film of oil on the spigot to aid in screwing the wood into the die chuck.

c) Leaving a square section on the wood, so that a wrench can be used to assist in screwing the wood into the chuck (I am not strong enough to rotate the wood by hand to screw it into the die chuck).

Next, place the end of the spigot into the entrance of the die chuck and bring up the tailstock to the other end. This helps make sure the threading of the wood is started straight. As the wood is rotated to screw the tenon into the die chuck, tighten the tailstock to help keep the stock true to the lathe axis.

Screw the tenon right into the die chuck, until the square shoulder on the wood firmly contacts the face of the die chuck. As with any threading operation using a die, it is important that you occasionally back off the wood to allow the die to clean up the threads properly.

It might even be a good idea to unscrew the wood from the die chuck, clean out any chips, lightly sand the wooden threads to remove any loose pieces, and re-oil the threaded tenon before screwing it back in to start turning. I also recommend the parting-off of the turned piece and leaving a square piece sticking out of the chuck to simplify removal of the threaded tenon from the chuck.

This form of chuck provides fairly positive repositioning of the work – if it has to be removed from the chuck before it is completed – so should be very good for production work, where the work cannot be completed without removing it from the lathe for some other operation; this is because the alignment of the workpiece to the chuck is at the mating

of the shoulder of the workpiece with the end of the die chuck.

The die chuck is sold with an optional Morse taper adapter, that screws into the threaded end of the chuck, allowing one to insert the adapter with a drive centre, and place the wood between centres to turn the $1\frac{1}{8}$in (28mm) tenon to screw into the die chuck. This is a nice touch, but I cannot see much saving in it because you have to unscrew the adapter from the chuck, before you can screw the wood into the chuck recess. I did find, however, that the Morse taper adapter screwed into the chuck provided an excellent extender to move the drive centre away from the headstock, which is useful for such operations as turning wooden spheres using a swinging cutter.

Suppliers and Manufacturers

Author's Note

The following list, in alphabetical order of country, was not designed to include every company in the world that sells woodturning supplies; it has been designed to help the reader find a particular tool that has been referenced in the text of Chapters 1 through 12. Manufacturers have been listed so that readers can contact them to locate a source nearest to them. In many cases, one can purchase directly from the manufacturer at their website. For the following items, I do not know of any supplier other than the manufacturer at this time: contact John Rea, for oval turning chuck; Sierra Mold Corporation, for the VacuuMaster Vacuum chuck; and Woodturner PRO, LLC, for the Longworth chuck and the doughnut chuck, which they are producing and selling.

AUSTRALIA

John Rea Attachments

T/A Cattell Investments Pty. Ltd
23 Fourth Avenue
Llandilo, NSW 2747
Australia

John Rea and Tom Cattell produce a decorative turning attachment for the wood lathe and an oval turning chuck. I believe these are made in limited production or on special order.

Tel: (02) 4777 5021 or (02) 4777 4224
Fax: (02) 4777 4225
E-mail: jrea@pnc.com.au

Vicmarc Machinery

52 Grice Street,
Clontarf, Qld 4350
Australia

Vicmarc Machinery manufactures a line of lathes and chucks and other items for holding wood on the lathe. Their Vacuum Plate is the simplest and least expensive vacuum chuck on the market.

Tel: 7 3284 3103 (in Australia)
Tel: +61 7 3284 3103 (Overseas)
Fax: 7 3283 4656 (in Australia)
Fax: +61 7 3283 4656 (Overseas)
E-mail: vicmarc@vicmarc.com
Website: http://www.vicmarc.com/

CANADA

Oneway Manufacturing

241 Monteith Ave
Stratford, Ontario N5A 2P6
Canada

Oneway Manufacturing produces some of the finest woodturning lathes in the world, a number of excellent four-jaw scroll chucks, and a number of other woodturning accessories applicable to holding wood on the lathe.

Toll Free: 1 800 565 7288 (within Canada and USA)
Tel: 1 519 271 7611
Fax: 1 519 271 8892

E-mail Oneway at any of the following addresses, whether it be product-related, service-related or any other question or query you might have about Oneway and their products:

Product Ordering: OrderDesk@oneway.ca
Technical Support: TechSupport@oneway.ca
General Enquiries: Postbox@oneway.ca
Website: http://www.oneway.ca

Woodchucker's Supplies

1698 Weston Road
Weston, Ontario M9N 1V6
Canada

Woodchucker's Supplies carry a number of woodturning tools and supplies and use the Craft Supplies Ltd in England catalogue as their own. I should note, however, that they do not stock all items.

Tel: 800 551 0192
E-mail: sales@woodchuckers.com
Website: http://www.woodchuckers.com

FRANCE

Jean-François Escoulen

Les Massots
26450 Puy Saint Martin
France

Jean-François Escoulen is a well-known French woodturner, who has developed a unique ball and socket chuck that provides a different approach to eccentric work. He divides his time between craft production, artistic creation and teaching.

Tel: 33 4 75 90 18 40
Fax: 33 4 75 90 42 35
E-mail: escoulen.jean-francois@wanadoo.fr
Website: http://www.escoulen.com

NEW ZEALAND

Kelton Industries Ltd
PO Box 589
Kaitaia 500
New Zealand

Kelton Industries Ltd is the company that produces the Kel McNaughton tools. Perhaps best known for their bowl saver used to core out bowl blanks to get more bowls from a block of wood.

Tel and Fax: NZ 9 408 5862
E-mail: info@kelton.co.nz
Website: http://www.kelton.co.nz/

Teknatool International

Mail Address:
PO Box 18-0034, Luckens Point
Henderson, Auckland 1008
New Zealand

Street Address:
65 The Concourse
Henderson, Auckland
New Zealand

Teknatool International manufacture the Nova line of lathes and chucks. Their products are distributed worldwide.

Tel: 0064 9 837 6900
Fax: 0064 9 837 6901
E-mail: sales@teknatool.com or service@teknatool.com
Website: http://www.teknatool.com

UNITED KINGDOM

Axminster Power Tool Centre

Chard Street
Axminster, Devon EX 13 5DZ
England

Axminster Power Tool Centre produces a wide range of woodworking tools including lathes and some of the finest chucks available.

Tel: 01297 35242
Telesales: 0900 371822
Technical Sales: 01297 33656
Customer Service: 0800 1699450
E-mail: email@axminster.co.uk
Website: http://www.axminster.co.uk

Craft Supplies Limited

The Mill, Millers Dale
Nr. Buxton, Derbyshire SK17 8SN
England

Craft Supplies Limited is a major supplier of woodturning tools and accessories. Many of the items mentioned in this book can be found in their catalogue or at their website.

Tel: +44 (0) 1298 871636
Fax: +44 (0) 1298 872263
E-mail: sales@craft-supplies.co.uk
Website: http://www.craft-supplies.co.uk

Mortimers' Woodturning & Patternmaking

Unit 3, Oakhurst Park
The Levels, Brereton
Rugeley, Staffs WS15 1RD
England

Bob Mortimer, of Mortimers' Woodturning and Patternmaking, is a professional woodturner who has developed a chuck to help with certain types of work. He calls it the Die Chuck, because it looks so much like a threading die.

E-mail: enquiries@mortimerswoodturning.com
Website: http://www.mortimerswoodturning.com

Multistar Woodturning Systems

4 Holledge Crescent

Frinton-on-Sea, Essex CO13 0RW

England

Tel: 01255 676026

Website: www.multistardirect.com

Peter Child Woodturning Supplies

The Old Hyde, Little Yeldham Road

Little Yeldham, Near Halstead, Essex CO9 4QT

England

This company supplies all sorts of woodturning accessories, including their exclusive Child coil chuck.

Tel: 01787 237291

Fax: 01787 238522

E-mail: sales@peterchild.co.uk

Website: http://www.peterchild.co.uk/

Record Power Limited

Parkway Works

Sheffield S9 3BL

England

Record Power are manufacturers of lathes and other woodworking power tools, a line of hand tools, and chucks and other accessories for holding wood on the lathe.

Tel: 0114 251 9102

Fax: 0114 261 7141

E-mail: recordpower@recordtools.co.uk

Website: http://www.recordpower.co.uk

Robert Sorby

Athol Road,

Sheffield S8 OPA

England

Robert Sorby is basically a manufacturer of hand tools, but does produce the eccentric chuck and other tools that may help hold wood on the lathe.

Tel: +44 114 225 0700

Fax: +44 114 225 0710

E-mail: sales@robert-sorby.co.uk

Website: http://www.robert-sorby.co.uk/

USA

The Beall Tool Company

541 Swans Road N.E.

Newark, Ohio 43055

USA

The Beall Tool Company is probably best known for its buffing system that mounts onto the spindle of the wood lathe and is used for finishing turned objects to a high shine. They also make a fine collet chuck that screws onto the spindle of the lathe and uses metal-lathe precision to hold wood on the lathe.

Tel: 1 800 331 4718

Fax: 740 345 5880

E-mail: jrbeall@bealltool.com

Website: http//www.bealltool.com/turning.htm

Best Wood Tools
1544 Milo Webb Drive
Crossville, TN 38572
USA

Best Wood Tools make a line of accessories for woodturning lathes and a number of items to help hold wood on the lathe. I've been using some of their spindle adapters for several years. They also make the line of Morse taper collet chucks. They have a line of faceplates and also a Tailstock chuck adapter that allows you to mount your chuck on the tailstock for aligning when applying to the vacuum chuck or to mount onto a faceplate using hot-melt glue.

Tel: 931 788 0429
Fax: 931 788 0450
E-mail: Sales@BestWoodTools.com
Website: http://www.BestWoodTools.com

Craft Supplies USA
1287 E 1120 S
Provo, UT 84608
USA

Craft Supplies USA is a major supplier of woodturning tools and accessories in the United States. Most of the items mentioned in this book may be ordered from their catalogue or from their website.

Tel: (800) 551 8876
FAX: 801 377 7742
E-mail: service@woodturnerscatalog.com
Website: http://www.woodturnerscatalog.com

Nichols Enterprises, Inc.
620 W Coe Ave
PO Box 936
Stanfield, OR 97875
USA

John Nichols of Nichols Enterprises, Inc. produces custom-built lathes and lathe accessories. The steady rest described and illustrated in Chapter 12 was made by John.

Tel: 541 449 1464
Fax: 541 449 1465
E-mail: lathebldr@aol.com
Website: http://www.nicholslathe.com

Packard Woodworks, Inc.
646 North Trade Street
Tryon, NC 28782
USA

Tel: (828) 859 6762
Fax: (828) 859 5551
E-mail: packard@alltel.nety
Website: www.packardwoodworks.com

Sierra Mold Corporation

1558 Forrest Way

Carson City, Nevada 89706

USA

The Sierra Mold Corporation manufacturers
the VacuuMaster vacuum chuck that does
not need a hole through the headstock
in order to operate.

Tel: (775) 882 3500

FAX: (775) 882 2502

E-mail: info@sierramold.com

Website: http://sierramold.com/

Woodturner PRO, LLC

14699 NE Prairie View Ct.

Aurora, OR 97002

USA

Woodturner PRO, LLC manufacture software
to aid in the design of segmented vessels;
they produce the Longworth chuck described
in Chapter 9, and the doughnut chuck
mentioned in Chapter 12.

Tel: 503 781 5117

E-mail: support@woodturnerpro.com

Website: http://www.woodturnerpro.com

About the Author

Fred Holder lives in Snohomish, Washington, USA with his wife Mildred; he has been turning wood since 1988. He does not specialize in any particular thing, but continues to experiment with different techniques. He has done quite a bit of segmented work; multi-centred work (using the Robert Sorby eccentric chuck and an Escoulen-type ball and socket chuck); bowls, both regular shaped and natural edge; making regular balls; making the Chinese

ball; hand-chasing of threads for boxes, walking stick joins, or any place where a threaded joint is needed – and a lot of other techniques. Fred is also proficient in the use of several thread-cutting jigs that are used in conjunction with the wood lathe and has used the tap and die and tap and screw box to cut threads in wood for many years.

He has demonstrated woodturning at fairs and exhibitions in the USA, Canada, New Zealand and the United Kingdom, and passes on his skills through teaching and writing. His articles have appeared in *American Woodturner*, *Woodturning* magazine, and *More Woodturning*, a monthly tabloid newspaper that he edits and publishes. Fred has been a member of the American Association of Woodturners (AAW) since 1991, and is a member of the National Association of Woodturners New Zealand; the International Wood Collectors' Society; of the National Wood Carvers' Association and the Seattle Chapter of AAW, and is past-president of the Northwest Washington Woodturners Chapter of AAW. Fred spearheaded the formation of this latter group in February 1996. Fred's website is at http://www.fholder.com/ and he can be reached by e-mail at woodturner@fholder.com.

This is Fred's second book. His first, *Making Screw Threads in Wood*, was also published by GMC Publications.

Index

TITLES AVAILABLE FROM
GMC Publications
BOOKS

CRAFTS

GARDENING

Tropical Garden Style with Hardy Plants *Alan Hemsley*
Water Garden Projects: From Groundwork to Planting *Roger Sweetinburgh*

PHOTOGRAPHY

Close-Up on Insects *Robert Thompson*
Digital Enhancement for Landscape Photographers
Arjan Hoogendam & Herb Parkin
Double Vision *Chris Weston & Nigel Hicks*
An Essential Guide to Bird Photography *Steve Young*
Field Guide to Bird Photography *Steve Young*
Field Guide to Landscape Photography *Peter Watson*
How to Photograph Pets *Nick Ridley*
In my Mind's Eye: Seeing in Black and White *Charlie Waite*
Life in the Wild: A Photographer's Year *Andy Rouse*

Light in the Landscape: A Photographer's Year *Peter Watson*
Photographers on Location with Charlie Waite *Charlie Waite*
Photography for the Naturalist *Mark Lucock*
Photojournalism: An Essential Guide *David Herrod*
Professional Landscape and Environmental Photography:
    From 35mm to Large Format *Mark Lucock*
Rangefinder *Roger Hicks & Frances Schultz*
Underwater Photography *Paul Kay*
Where and How to Photograph Wildlife *Peter Evans*
Wildlife Photography Workshops *Steve & Ann Toon*

ART TECHNIQUES

Oil Paintings from your Garden: A Guide for Beginners *Rachel Shirley*

VIDEOS

Drop-in and Pinstuffed Seats *David James*
Stuffover Upholstery *David James*
Elliptical Turning *David Springett*
Woodturning Wizardry *David Springett*
Turning Between Centres: The Basics *Dennis White*
Turning Bowls *Dennis White*
Boxes, Goblets and Screw Threads *Dennis White*
Novelties and Projects *Dennis White*
Classic Profiles *Dennis White*

Twists and Advanced Turning *Dennis White*
Sharpening the Professional Way *Jim Kingshott*
Sharpening Turning & Carving Tools *Jim Kingshott*
Bowl Turning *John Jordan*
Hollow Turning *John Jordan*
Woodturning: A Foundation Course *Keith Rowley*
Carving a Figure: The Female Form *Ray Gonzalez*
The Router: A Beginner's Guide *Alan Goodsell*
The Scroll Saw: A Beginner's Guide *John Burke*

MAGAZINES

WOODTURNING ◆ WOODCARVING ◆ FURNITURE & CABINETMAKING
THE ROUTER ◆ NEW WOODWORKING ◆ THE DOLLS' HOUSE MAGAZINE
OUTDOOR PHOTOGRAPHY ◆ BLACK & WHITE PHOTOGRAPHY
MACHINE KNITTING NEWS ◆ KNITTING
GUILD OF MASTER CRAFTSMEN NEWS

The above represents a full list of all titles currently published or scheduled to be published.
All are available direct from the Publishers or through bookshops, newsagents and specialist retailers.
To place an order, or to obtain a complete catalogue, contact:

GMC Publications,
Castle Place, 166 High Street, Lewes, East Sussex BN7 1XU United Kingdom
Tel: 01273 488005 Fax: 01273 402866
E-mail: pubs@thegmcgroup.com

Orders by credit card are accepted